Deutsche Grammatik
für
A1 bis B2

Language is a reflection of Time, Place and Society, hence, its also a means to know about the country its people, rituals and habits- "Deutsch lernen Deutschland kennelmen"
The German is very easy if you learn it the right way and difficult if you try to learn it through short cuts. Let this be clear there is no short cut to learning only, shorter methods to learn. Pass your A1, A2 and B1 and B2 level examination in 3 months only. Required is just will power and enough interest to follow and practice the suggestions in the book. This book is good for both the teachers and the students, who often have to search and waste time and energy for „what should be taught?" or „What all I must learn" to clear my certifications. Pass your A1, A2 and B1 and B2 level examination in 3 months only. Required is just a sincere approach and enough interest to follow and practice the suggestions in the book. The book is good for both the teachers and the students, who often have to search and waste time and energy for „what should be taught?" or „What all I must learn" to clear my certifications. There has been a tremendous change in methods of learning and teaching a language over the years. In developed countries, the cost books and access to modern learning systems still come at a huge cost, despite the availability. Besides the pressure of learning quickly has risen with demand in making oneself available for the opportunity. This may arise out of travel requirement, receive a client or altogether to present oneself as a prospective candidate at the knock of the hour. This book offers a solution to those who wish to take the capsule approach to cut down on the learning curve by saving both on investments in the form of time and money. Sincere effort is still required with some guidance German can be mastered in a matter of just 3 months.

Abhay [askki] Singh [askki@outlook.com]

WIDMUNG

„Meine Liebe zu dir wird niemals abnehmen,
meine Mutter wirst du mich doch verstehn.
Du bist das Wichtigste in meinem Leben,
ich würde alles für dich abgeben.
Du machst mich zur glücklichsten Sohn der Welt,
ein Band, das für immer und ewig hält.
Ich hab dich lieb, meine Mutter.“

Vorwort

The purpose of putting the learnings in this book, a pragmatic approach has been adapted rather methodical. Approach of learning through the prescribed books and face-to-face, which is cost and time intensive, which is not as conducive to many societies.

A sincere approach and enough interest to follow and practice the suggestions in the book will help you through A1, A2 and B1 and B2 levels examination within 3 months.

This book   will come handy both to the teachers and the students alike, who often have to search and waste time and energy for „what should be taught? " or „What shall I learn?" to clear my certificate exams.
This knowledge capsule will guide you step by step in a pragmatic approach
There has been a tremendous change in methods of teaching a a language over the years.
In developing countries the cost books and access to modern learning systems is comes at a huge cost, despite the availability.
Besides, the pressure of learning quickly has risen with demand in makeing oneself available for the opportunity.

This book is the solution for those who wish to take the capsule approach to cut down on the learning curve by saving both on investments in time and money. I assure you that German can be mastered in a matter of just 3 months.
DANKSAGUNG

An dieser Stelle möchte ich mich bei all denjenigen bedanken, die mich während der Anfertigung dieses Buch unterstützt und motiviert haben.
Zuerst gebührt mein Dank Frau Dr. Ina Schmelzer. Sie hat das Buch Begutachtet. Für die hilfreichen Anregungen und die konstruktive Kritik bei der Erstellung dieser Arbeit möchte ich mich herzlich bedanken.
Ich bedanke mich bei meinem Projekt Leiter bei IBM, India, Herr Sham Dhage, für die moralische Unterstützung and Motivierung.
Ein besonderer Dank gilt auch allen Freunden und Bekannten die Familie eingeschlossen, ohne die diese Arbeit nicht hätte entstehen können.
Bedanken möchte ich mich für die zahlreichen interessanten Ideen und Inputs, die maßgeblich dazu beigetragen haben, daß dieses Buch in dieser Form vorliegt.

Abhay Singh
Pune, 10.05.2020

Table of Contents

Das Alphabet = The Alphabets

a	b	c	d	e		f	g	h		i	j	k	l	m		n	o	p	q	r	s	t	u		v		w	x	y	z

	ä	ü	ö	ß	

A a	**B b**	**C c**	**D d**	**E e**	**F f**	**G g**	**H h**	**I i**
aa	*bey*	*zey*	*dey*	*a*	*eff*	*gey*	*ha*	*ee*
J j	**K k**	**L l**	**M m**	**N n**	**O o**	**P p**	**Q q**	**R r**
yott	*ka*	*ell*	*em*	*en*	*o*	*pey*	*ku*	*er*
S s	**T t**	**U u**	**V v**	**W w**	**X x**	**Y y**	**Z z**	
es	*tey*	*u*	*fau*	*wey*	*iks*	*yupsilon*	*zett*	

The letters have been divided in 3 groups:

Konsonanten = Mitlaute (consonants)

Vokale = Selbstlaute (vowels)

Umlaute (umlaute)

Konsonanten (consonants)	b, c, d, f, g, h, j, k, l, m, n, p, q, r, s, t, v, w, x, y, z, ß
Vokale (vowels)	a, e, i, o, u
Umlaute (umlaute)	ä, ö, ü

Instead of the "Umlaut" and the "ß" you can just write:

ä = ae   Ä = Ae   ö = oe   Ö = Oe
ue = ü   Ue = Ü   ß = ss

Or, you use the shortcuts on your English (qwerty) keyboard to write:

ä	ALT + 0228
Ä	ALT + 0196
ö	ALT + 0246
Ö	ALT + 0214
ü	ALT + 0252
Ü	ALT + 0220
ß	ALT + 0223

The Pronounciation

Laut	Erklärung	Beispiele
ch	und, To speak it out: - press your tongue on the bottom of your mouth, - close the gap between the upper and - lower part of your mouth then - try to blow out air between the remaining little gap.	mich ich dich durch
ch	**Strong sounds**	Macht Achtung auch noch
Sch	Always pronounced as English - **Sh**	Schule Schokolade schreiben
ie	The "ie" is spoken like the German "i" - very easy. It's a long "i".	Lied Liebe Liege

		viel
ei	The "ei" is spoken like the English word "I" - very easy.	Ei mein schein beide
e	In German you must mind that all alphabets are spoken. It sounds as if you didn't understand somebody and you ask with "hey"? Be ware.	Auge Liebe Rose Danke
r	Roll the "r" a bit loud and clear.	Rose raus richtig
ck	The "ck" sounds more as the English"k".	Glück locken schicken
au	The "au" its an easy sound.	Auto Maus aus
eu	The "eu" sounds a bit like the "oiiii".	euch Europa Feuer
z	+ o i e u - pronounced as „tS" in English. Its a dental sound	zu Zeit Zahn Zoo
s	At the beginning of the word and followed by consonants will pronounced as in „English"	Syllable syllabus Stern
s	+ o i e u - pronounced as „J" in English	Sonne Sohn Sahne sein
ß / ß	This letter ß, is called "eszett", and pronounced as English's', Always pronounced as English „s"	Straße Snorkel beißen
v	The „v" sounds like „f"	Volk von viel verliebt
v	„Foreign words" with – the letter V will be pronounced **as in original form in English** and the rest of the word will be pronounced as in German language.	Volt, Video, Visa, Vitamin

Spellings: Upper and Lower Case

Note that the pronoun ich ('I') has no initial capital in German, but „Sie" she (formal form of 'you') has.

Upper Case	Lower Case
Beginning of a sentence	Verbs with an article
Names and proper names	Adjectives
Nouns	Noun + adjective
Adjective with an article or quantity - adjectives	Verbs

Write the beginning of a sentence with a capital letter.
example(s)

Ich habe zwei Keinder. Sie heißen Christine und Anna.

Karsten ist 16 Jahre alt. Anna ist erst 13.

Er ist 13 Jahre alt. Sie wird bald 14.

Word Order

Word order is much more flexible in German than in English, but there are some very important rules. The most important apply to the position of the finite *verb*. Here are some basic principles, which illustrate the difference to English word order.

The finite verb is *the second idea* in most statements:

Er *hat* zwei Brüder.	He has two brothers.

| rgen *fahre* ich nach Manchester. | Tomorrow I'm going to Manchester. |

The finite verb goes at the beginning of a sentence in orders and many questions:

Öffnet das Fenster!   Open the window, please. Hast Du morgen Zeit?   Are you free tomorrow?

The finite verb goes at the end in subordinate clauses:

Ich kann morgen nicht kommen, weil ich nach Manchester fahre. I can't come tomorrow because I'm going to Manchester.
If there are two verb forms, one of them goes at the end:

Morgen *muss* ich nach Manchester *fahren.*
Tomorrow I have to go to Manchester.

<u>Clue(s)</u>
A sentence starts with a capital letter

Names and proper names <u>will always</u> start with a capital letter.
Example(s)

Ich bin Karsten.
Wir gehen nach Haus.
Die Schule ist sehr weit.

Clue(s)
Further examples for proper names are:
Ich liebe den Stillen Gegend.

Wir fliegen in die Vereinigten Staaten von Amerika.

Sie treffen sich am Brandeburgertor.

Proper nouns start with a capital letter, even though if parts of the proper nouns are adjectives.
Further examples for proper nouns are:
Ich liebe das Berliner Brötchen.

Der Hamburger Hafen ist sehr Groß.
Hast den Großen Bären gesehen?
Nouns always start with a capital letter.
example(s)
Thomas liebt Christine.
Thomas will Christine heiraten.
Das Mädchen ist hübsch.
Clue(s)
Nouns are all things you can touch.
Typical endings of nouns are:
-nis (das Hindernis, die Erlaubnis, das Geständnis, ...)

-sis (die Basis, die Dosis, die Skepsis, ...)
-kit (die Kleinigkit, die Schwierigkit, die Haltbarkit, ...)
-schaft (die Freundschaft, die Herrschaft, die Meisterschaft, ...)
-tät (die Realität, die Qualität, ...)
-ion (die Tradition, die Dimension, ...)
-heit (die Gesundheit, die Freiheit, die Dummheit, ...)
-ung (die Erfahrung, die Meinung, die Werbung, ...)

Nouns are words which have a definite article (der, die, das) or an indefinite article (ein, eine).
Nouns can occur as subject or as an object.

Write adjectives in small letters. Berlin ist eine Teure teure Stadt.
Die Frauen essen die gelbe Blätter.
Er liebt Gute gute Bücher.

Clue(s)
An adjective is a word which describes a noun. It shows how something or somebody is (nice, fast, blue ...).
Adjectives + article or "quantity-adjectives" - Capital letter.
example(s)
Das Beste daran ist die Schokolade.
Mir gefällt das Rote Kleid.
Er hat das Richtige getan.

Clue(s)
If an adjective starts with a capital letter when its used as „Substantive"
(nominalizations).

The easiest way to recognize a noun are the articles (das | der |die).

Sometimes the possessive (e.g. in) and article are joined together: in + das = ins.

e.g. Er hat ins Schwarze getroffen. (Do you recognize the article?)

Besides articles you can recognize nominalizations with the help of words like viel, wenig, alles,
etwas, nichts (adjectives, that describe quantities):
Er hat nichts Wichtiges.
Er wird etwas Gutes tun.
Dann passierte etwas Ungewöhnliches während der Hochzeit.

A word consists of a noun + adjective - Small letters.
Die Stadt ist ~~Menschenleer~~ menschenleer.
Ich bin ~~Urlaubsreif~~ urlaubsreif.

Clue (s)
Sometimes, you have adjectives consisting of a noun and an adjective. Together, they form a new
adjective and are written small.
If necessary, there might be an s in between to join them.

In the 3rd example Menschen is the noun (everything you can do). Leer is an adjective (=how is
something?).

Write verbs in small letters.

Der Lehrer ~~Zeigt~~ zeigt den Schülern die neuen Bücher.
(The teacher is showing the books to the students.)
Ich ~~Beantworte~~ beantworte gerne eure Fragen.
(I'd like to answer your questions.)

Sie ~~Läuft~~ läuft in die Stadt.   (She is walking into the city.)
Clue(s)
Zeigen, beantworten, laufen and so on are all verbs (=everything you can touch) => small letters
exception(s)

Verbs that follow an article start with a capital letter and denote a Noun.
Das lachen ~~Lachen~~ tut ihm gut.
(Laughing is good for him.)

Dieses warten ~~Warten~~ macht mich noch verrückt.
(That waiting drives me crazy.)

Vom lesen ~~Lesen~~ bekomme ich Kopfschmerzen.
(I get a headache reading the book.)

<u>Clue(s)</u>

If a verb starts with capital letter we speak about the so-called "Substantivierung" (nominalizations).
The easiest way to recognize it are the articles (der|die|das).

Sometimes the posessive(e.g. *bei*) and article are joined together: *bei*+*dem* = **beim**.
Viel Spaß **beim** Bieten. (Happy bidding!) In this case you can't recognize the article easily.
Another example is: *von* + *dem* = **vom**. Vom Lesen bekomme ich Kopfschmerzen (I get a headache reading the book.).

Overview Parts of Speech

German	English	Examples
Nomen (=Substantiv) Konkrete Nomen Abstrakte Nomen	Noun (= noun) Proper nouns Abstract nouns	Haus, Hund, Stein, Möbel, Rose, Hand *(...was materiel ist)* Liebe, Freude, Freundschaft, Haß, Mut, Stärke, Hilfe *(...was nicht materiel ist)*
Artikel Bestimmter Artikel maskulin feminin neuter	Article Definite article masculine feminine neutral	Der, Die das der (= Singular), die (= Plural) der (= Singular and plural), das (= Singular), die (= Plural)
Adjektiv	Adjective	gut, Schön, groß, treu, rot, blau, weiß ...
Partizip Präsens Perfekt Prat Futur	Participle (Tense) Present Indefinite Perfect Past Future	Lachen, hoffen, lieben, glauben, schreiben, lesen gelacht, gehofft, geliebt, ge.glaubt, geschrieben, gelesen
Verb Hauptverb Hilfsverb Modalverb	Main verb helping verb Modal verb	lesen, schreiben, üben, lieben, hassen, prüfen, laufen, sein, haben, werden wollen, sollen, müßen, mögen, dürfen
Adverb lokal temporal modal kausal	Adverb Local temporal modal causal	hier, dort, da, bergauf heute, morgen, bald gern, vielleicht, ebenso darum, deshalb, vorsichtshalber
Präposition	Prepostion	in, im, auf, unter, über, zwischen, mitten, hinauf, hinab, diesseits, jenseits .. gegenüber, Entlang,
Numerale Bestimmtes Numerale Unbestimmtes Numerale Sonstige Numerale	 Specific numeric word Indefinite numeric word Other Numerales	ein, zwei, drei ... alles, nichts, wenig, viel, manches, einiges, etwas einfach, zweifach ... einmal, zweimal ...
Pronomen Personalpronomen Reflexivpronomen Demonstrativpronomen Possessivpronomen Relativpronomen Interrogativpronomen	Pronouns Personal pronouns Reflexive pronouns Demonstrative ronouns possessive pronouns relative pronouns Interrogative pronouns	ich, du, er, sie, es, wir ihr, sie mich, dich, sich der, die, das *(betont!)* (emphasize!) mein, dein, sein, ihr, euer, unser Wer? Was? Wie? Welcher? Welche? Welches? Woher? Wohin? Weshalb? Wieso?
Konjunktion Nebenordnende Unterordnende	Conjunction Associated conjunctions Subordinate conjunctions	und, zudem, außerdem, sowohl - als auch, oder, entweder - oder als, wenn, weil, da, damit, so daß, obwohl
Interjektion	Exclamation word	Aua! Ach! Hallo! Oh! Hoppla!

Inflectable {adj}   ***non-* inflectable {adj}**

declinable   Conjugable   -
Noun   *Verb*   *Adverb*
Article   *Preposition*
Pronoun   *Conjunction*
Numerals   *interjection*

Übersicht über die Wortarten

Wortarten

flektierbare   **nicht flektierbare**

deklinierbare   konjugierbare

* Nomen   * Verb   * Adverb
* Artikel   * Präposition
* Pronomen   * Konjunktion
* Numerale   * Interjektion
* Adjektiv

Adjective

Genders

There are masculine, feminine or neuter genders. This is similar to Hindi and Marathi language
This will be visible through singular article:

der   - masculine,   **die**   - feminine,   **das**   - neutral

We must understand that gender is used for grammatical purposes, i.e. the genders may not (always)
necessarily represent the actual gender (as in biology), this is contradictory to our understanding of the
genders.
This means that objects and ideas can be masculine, feminine or neutral:

der **Tisch**   the table (*masculine*)
die **Tür**   the door (*feminine*)
as **Fenster**   the window (*neuter*)

Declension in German Grammar -- The four Cases

The four cases in German grammar are nominative (subject), accusative (direct object), dative (indirect
object) and genitive (possessive). Because the word order of sentences is not fixed in German grammar, we
need the cases to tell us what role a noun or pronoun is playing in a sentence. Articles, nouns, adjectives and
pronouns all have to be declined or inflected to reflect a case.

German Cases, Articles & Adjectives

Below you will find tables and explanations regarding the use of the four German cases (Nominative,
Accusative, Genitive & Dative). In order to be able to use these tables correctly, it is important for you to
know the gender of the German nouns you learn (German nouns can be feminine, masculine or neuter).
Knowing the gender means that you know which article to use in the table. Articles change depending on
which of the four the cases is being used.
To learn new German nouns along with their base articles (der / die / das), check out our vocabulary section.
To learn some new German adjectives that we can use with these nouns, check out our adjectives section.
German adjectives are learned in their simple form (alt, jung, laut, klein), but become influenced by various
factors when used in a sentence. These factors include the gender of the noun they are describing, and the
case that is applied to them (depending on the context of the sentence). These changes involve adding certain
endings to the adjectives, which are marked in the tables below in bold.

Artikel - Wie gehts denn hier?

Hast du Problem mit den deutschen artikeln?

Es gibt dutzende, verschiedene Endungen, die dir den richtigen Artikel verraten können! Schaffst du es
einfach nicht, dir alle zu merken? **Kein** Problem!

Ich habe das Rad nicht neu erfunden, aber mit Hilfe dieses einfachen Tricks wirst du im Schnitt 75% aller Wörter richtig raten! Je mehr der allgemeinen Merkmale (Endung, biologisches Geschlecht, Bedeutung), die den Artikel bestimmen, du kennst, um so näher wirst du an die 100% rankommen!

DER ARTIKELTRICK:
Der Artikeltrick basiert auf den obigen Wahrscheinlich**kit**en und den allgemeinen Merkmalen, mit denen du den Artikel bestimmen kannst.
Die realistische Wahrscheinlich**kit**en für die 3 Artikel

der	die	das
41%	35%	24%

1. Personen sind immer männlich und Tiere FAST immer (außer du spricht ganz explizit über eine Frau → Endung –in oder -frau oder ein weibliches Tier)
2. Tippe bei den Endungen „chen", „lein" und „ment" auf „das"
3. Tippe bei allen Wörtern die auf „e", „heit", „**kit**", „ung" „schaft" und „ion" enden auf „die"
4. Tippe bei allen anderen auf maskulin

Mehr ist es nicht! Du musst „nur" 3 neutrale und 6 feminine Endungen lernen und beachten, daß Personen immer maskulin sind, außer es sind Frauen. Für alles andere tippst du auf Grund der Wahrscheinlichkiten einfach auf „der".
Ausnahmen sind oft neutral, also „das", je besser du dich mit den Regeln für neutrale Nomen auskennst, um so besser wirst du die Artikel raten.

PS: Die Regeln für maskuline Nomen kannst du Weglassen! Da du im Zweifel ja eh auf maskulin tippst! Lerne zusätzlich zu den Regeln des Artikeltricks nur die Regeln für feminine und neutrale Nomen. // Es geht auch nicht darum, daß der Trick IMMER funktioniert, das tut er nicht, aber er soll dir die Angst vor den Artikeln nehmen!

ARTIKEL – DEKLINATION IST EINFACH!
Du brauchst nicht gefühlt hunderte verschiedene Endungen und Tabellen!!
Du brauchst nur eine Tabelle,:

	Nominativ	Akkusativ	Dativ	Genitiv
Maskulin	der Mann	den Mann	dem Mann	des Mannes
Feminin	die Frau	die Frau	der Frau	der Frau
Neutral	das Keind	das Keind	dem Keind	des Keindes
Plural	die Eltern	die Eltern	den Eltern	der Eltern

Ich bin mir sicher, daß du diese Tabelle schon kennst, oder?
Warum brauchst du nur diese, wenn dir dein Lehrer bisher so viele verschiedene gezeigt hat?

Nun die Endungen sind immer gleich! Falls du bis heute das System dahinter noch nicht gesehen hast, zeige ich es dir jetzt!

Unbestimmte Artikel:

	Nominativ	Akkusativ	Dativ	Genitiv
Maskulin	der ein	den einen	dem einem	des eines
Feminin	die eine	die eine	der einer	der einer
Neutral	das ein	das ein	dem einem	des eines
Plural	die	Die	Den	der

Siehst du das System? Du mußt nur wissen, welche Form gar keine Endung benutzt! Alle anderen Endungen sind gleich! Schauen wir uns noch mehr Artikel an!

Der Negativartikel:

	Nominativ	Akkusativ	Dativ	Genitiv
Maskulin	der kein	den **keinen**	dem **keinem**	des **keines**
Feminin	die **keine**	die **keine**	der **keiner**	der **keiner**
Neutral	das **kein**	das **kein**	dem **keinem**	des **keines**
Plural		die **keine**	die **keine**	der **keiner**

Die Possessivartikel

Personalpronomen	Possessivartikel
ich	mein
du	dein
er	sein
sie	ihr
es	sein
wir	unser
ihr	euer
sie (Pl.)	ihr
Sie (formal)	Ihr

Spätestens jetzt solltest du das System dahinter erkennen! Du mußt nur wissen, daß im Nominativ Maskulin, Nominativ Neutral und Akkusativ Neutral gar **keine** Endung benutzt werden.

Bei allen anderen fügst du einfach die Endung des bestimmten Artikels hinzu!

Bestimmter Artikel

Definte article : "the" of English				
	Mas	Neutral	Feminin	Plural
Nominativ	der	das	die	die
Akkusativ	den	das	die	die
Dativ	dem	dem	der	den -n
Genetive	des -s / -es	des -s / -es	der	der

Unbestimmter Artikel

Indefinite Article: a /an of English		this is Singular form, hence , no plurals		
	Mas	Neutral	Feminin	Plural
Nominativ	ein	ein	eine	
Akkusativ	einen	ein	eine	
Dativ	einem	einem	einer	
Genetive	eines -s/ es	eines -s/ es	einer	none

Negativ Artikel

Indefinite Article: A /an of English this is the Singular Form, hence, no Plurals

	Mas	Neutral	Feminin	Plural
Nominativ	**kein**	**kein**	**keine**	**keine**
Akkusativ	**keinen**	**kein**	**keine**	**keine**
Dativ	**keinem**	**keinem**	**keiner**	**keinen -n**
Genetive	**keines** -s/ es	**keines** -s/ es	**keiner**	**keiner**

Nominative case - Definite Article:

The nominative case is used for the subject of the sentence. The subject of the sentence is the person or thing doing something. For example:

Der Hund ißt das Brot. – [The dog eats the bread]

Der alte Hund ißt das Brot. – [The old dog eats the bread]

Who is doing the action in this sentence?   The dog.

This makes "Der Hund" the subject of the sentence, meaning that the article belonging to "Hund" (der because it is a masculine noun) and any adjectives describing "Hund" (alt) must comply with the rules for the nominative case.

These rules can be seen in the table below:

The same rules apply if the subject of the sentence has an indefinite article (ein / eine / ein): For example:
Eine Katze trinkt die Milch. – [A cat drinks the milk].
Eine kleine Katze trinkt die Milch. – [A small cat drinks the milk].
The cat is doing the action (it is drinkeing the milk), so the article belonging to "Katze" (eine because it is a feminine noun) and any adjectives describing "Katze" (klein) will follow the rules of the nominative case:

Masculine	Feminine	Neuter	Plural
ein	Eine	ein	keine
ein alter Hund	eine kleine Katze	ein großes Haus	keine bunten Blumen

No Article

If the subject of the sentence has no article, the following changes happen to the adjective:
Frisches Brot schmeckt gut. – [Fresh bread tastes good].
The adjectives will take on the endings of the missing articles, as you can see in the following table:

Masculine	Feminine	Neuter	Plural
heißer Kaffee	kalte Milch	frisches Brot	warme Brötchen

**Note: The verb "sein" acts like an equals sign (=) in a sentence, which means that anything on the other side of "sein" is still in the same case as the subject:
Der Hund ist ein alter Freund von mir. –
The dog is an old friend of mine.
Both "Der Hund" and "ein alter Freund" are the subjects of the sentence because the dog is both; it is a dog and it is an old friend of mine. Therefore, both nouns, their articles, and their adjectives must follow the rules of the nominative case.
The nominative case is the basic form for articles, adjectives, nouns, and pronouns. The subject of the sentence is always in the nominative case. We can find the nominative by askeing wer/was - Who/what is performing the action?
Example:
Das kleine Haus gehört dem freundlichen Mann.
Es gehört dem freundlichen Mann.

Accusative Case

Maskuline	Feminine	Neuter	Plural
den	die	das	die
den alten Hund	die kleine Katze	das große Haus	die bunten Blumen

Maskuline	Feminine	Neuter	Plural
einen	eine	ein	keine
einen alten Hund	eine kleine Katze	ein großes Haus	keine bunten Blumen

Maskuline	Feminine	Neuter	Plural
heißen Kaffee	kalte Milch	frisches Brot	warme Brötchen

The accusative case follows certain verbs and prepositions, we can find it by asking wen/was – Whom/what is the direct recipient of the action?
Example:
Ich kenne den freundlichen Mann schon seit vielen Jahren.
Ich kenne ihn schon seit vielen Jahren.

Dative Case
The dative case follows certain verbs and prepositions, we can find by asking the question wem / was – To whom/what is indirect action of the verb being directed?
Example:
Das kleine Haus gehört dem freundlichen Mann.
Das kleine Haus gehört ihm.

Maskuline	Feminine	Neuter	Plural
dem	der	dem	den
dem alten Hund	der kleinen Katze	dem großen Haus	den bunten Schuhen*

Maskuline	Feminine	Neuter	Plural
einem	einer	einem	keinen
einem alten Hund	einer kleinen Klatze	einem großen Haus	keinen bunten Schuhen*

Maskuline	Feminine	Neuter	Plural
heißem Kaffee	kalter Milch	frischem Brot	warmen Brötchen

Genitive Case

The genitive case shows possession/belonging. The genitive is also used after certain prepositions, verbs, and adjectives.

Example:
Das Haus des freundlichen Mannes steht unweit unseres Hauses.

Maskuline	Feminine	Neuter	Plural
des	der	des	der
des alten Hundes*	der kleinen Katze	des großen Hauses*	der bunten Schuhe

Maskuline	Feminine	Neuter	Plural
eines	einer	eines	keiner
eines alten Hundes*	einer kleinen Katze	eines großen Hauses*	keiner bunten Schuhe

Maskuline	Feminine	Neuter	Plural
heißen Kaffees*	kalter Milch	frischen Brotes*	warmer Brötchen

Genitive, Dative, Accusative
Here you will find a list of prepositions – and some important verbs – that take the genitive, dative, or accusative. I will also explain when to use certain prepositions (auf, hinter, vor, ...) with either the dative or accusative.
Example:Der Mann steht außerhalb seines kleinen Hauses. (Genitive)
Er steht vor seinem kleinen Haus. (Dative)
Er stellt sich vor sein kleines Haus. (Akkusative)

Pronouns

Aim of this section is to learn the personal pronouns and their use in the four cases.
There are several types of pronouns:
Personalpronomen (personal pronoun): replaces a noun or refers back to a noun

Possessivpronomen (possessive pronoun): a word that shows to whom something belongs

Demonstrativpronomen (demonstrative pronoun): a word to point out a particular thing or person

Reflexivpronomen (reflexive pronoun): if subject and object (=here the pronoun) are the same person the pronoun is called "Reflexivpronomen". It reflects back to the noun.

Relativpronomen (relative pronoun): introduces a relative clause and refers back to the noun of the main sentence

Fragepronomen (interrogative pronoun): is a question word which is used to ask for a pronoun

Indefinitpronomen (indefinite pronoun): is a pronoun which refers to somebody or something in general - not a particular one

General Rules

The term personal comes from word person. We use the personal pronouns to talk about a person or thing.

The term pronoun consists of the words pro (für) and noun (nomen) which means the pronouns stand for a person / thing and with their help the name of the noun can be replaced.

For ex.: Thomas is my friend. He lives in Berlin (instead of repeating the name again: My friend Thomas lives in Berlin).

All personal Pronouns:

Person	Numerus	Geschlecht	Nominativ		Genitiv		Dativ		Akkusativ	
			Deutsch	Englisch	Deutsch	Englisch	Deutsch	Englisch	Deutsch	Englisch
1. Person	Singular	-	ich	I	mein(e/er)	my	mir	me	mich	me
2. Person	Singular	-	du	you	dein(e/er)	your	dir	you	dich	you
3. Person	Singular	männlich	er	he	sein(e/er)	his	ihm	him	ihn	him
3. Person	Singular	weiblich	sie	she	ihr(e/er)	her	ihr	her	sie	her
3. Person	Singular	sächlich	es	it	sein(e/er)	its	ihm	it	es	it
1 .Person	Plural	-	wir	we	unser(e)	our	uns	us	uns	us
2. Person	Plural	-	ihr	you	euer(e)	your	euch	you	euch	you
3. Person	Plural	-	sie	they	ihr(e/er)	their	ihnen	them	sie	them
2 .Person	Sing /Plu	-	Sie	You (formal)	Ihr(e/er)	your	Ihnen	you	Sie	you

1. Person: pronouns of the 1st person refer to the speaker
2. Person: pronouns of the 2nd person refer to the person you are talkeing to
3. Person: pronouns of the 3rd person refer to the person / thing you are talkeing about

Personal pronouns in nominative

These pronouns are used to speak about a person / thing who does something or is something. The pronoun is the subject of the sentence.

ich: you use when you speak <u>about</u> yourself

du: you use when you speak <u>to</u> a single person (informal)

er: you use when you speak <u>about</u> a male person or a thing with a male gender

sie: you use when you speak <u>about</u> a female person or a thing with a female gender

es: you use when you speak <u>about</u> a thing with a neutral gender

wir: you use when you speak <u>about</u> several people yourself included

ihr: you use when you speak <u>to</u> several people

sie: you use when you speak <u>about</u> several people

Sie: you use when you speak <u>to</u> a single person (formal)

There are two big differences between German and English:
- In German "er/sie" (he/she) is also used to describe dead things. Most dead things in German have a male or female gender.
- In German are two forms of "you". "Du" is used for family members, friends, children and other people who are close to the speaker. "Sie" is formal way to say you and is used for business partner, colleagues and other adults who are not close to the speaker.

Personal pronouns in dative and accusative

Here you can use the same explanation like in nominative. We speak again about a person / thing but in the dative and accusative the person / thing is not acting. It is the object of the sentence.

Surely you will ask where is the difference between dative and accusative because in English there is just one case and not two. This is an own big topic and will be covered in the section "Die 4 Fälle".

mir / mich: you use when somebody does something with you

dir / dich: you use when you do something with a single person (informal)

ihm / ihn: you use when somebody does something with a male person

ihr / sie: you use when somebody does something with a female person

ihm / es: you use when somebody does something with a dead thing

uns / uns: you use when somebody does something with several people yourself included

euch / euch: you use when somebody does something with several people

ihnen / sie : you use when somebody does something with several people

Ihnen / Sie: you use when you do something with a single person (formal)

Personal Pronouns in Genitive
The personal pronouns in genitive are not used to talk about the person but about what belongs to the person / about what poßeßes the person.
mein(e/er): you use to talk about things which belong to you

dein(e/er): you use to talk about things which belong to a single person (informal)

sein(e/er): you use to talk about things which belong to a male person

ihr(e/er): you use to talk about things which belong to a female person

sein(e/er): you use to talk about things which belong to a dead thing

unser(e): you use to talk about things which belong several people yourself included

euer(e) : you use to talk about things which belong to several people

ihr(e/er) : you use to talk about things which belong to several people

Ihr(e/er): you use to talk about things which belong to a single person (formal)

I put the endings in brackets because in the genitive case it depends on the gender which ending you have to use. This problem will be covered in the section "Possessivpronomen".

Possessiv Pronomen

Possessivpronomen sind mein, dein, sein, ihr, unser, euer, ihr und die jeweils deklinierten Formen. Sie ersetzen ein bereits genanntes Nomen und zeigen den Besitz oder die Zugehörigkit zu diesem Nomen an.

Sie müssen dekliniert werden.

Beispiele:

„Ist das dein Koffer?" – „Ja, das ist meiner!"

„Wem gehört die Katze?" – „Das ist meine!"

The term personal comes from word person. We use the personal pronouns to talk about a person or thing. The term pronoun consists of the words pro (für) and noun (Nomen) which means the pronouns stand for a person / thing and with their help the name of the noun can be replaced.

example: Catherine Rudolf is my girlfriend. She lives in Cagayan (instead of repeating the name again: Catherine Rudolf lives in Cagayan.)).
Personal pronouns in Nominative

These pronouns are used to speak about a person / thing who does something or is something. The pronoun is the subject of the sentence.

The meaning of the possessive pronouns can be explained with one little table:

person	numerus	gender	German	English
1st person	singular	-	mein	my
2nd person	singular	-	dein	your
3rd person	singular	male	sein	his
3rd person	singular	female	ihr	her
3rd person	singular	neuter	sein	its
1st person	plural	-	unser	our
2nd person	plural	-	euer	your
3rd person	plural	-	ihr	their
2nd person (formal)	singular / plural	-	Ihr	your

For example 1: **Mein** Freund heißt Tom. (My boyfriend is called Tom.)

- gender of "Freund": male
- numerus of "Freund": singular
- case of "Freund" here: nominative
  ("Freund" is the subject of the sentence => nominative)

If you look for singular, male, nominative you'll find no ending. So it must be "Mein Freund".

example 2:

Ich besuche **meinen** Freund. (I visit my friend.)

- gender of "Freund": male
- numerus of "Freund": singular
- case of "Freund" here: accusative ("Ich" is the subject. "Freund" is the direct object of the sentence =>case)

If you look for singular, male, accusative you'll find the ending "en". So it must be "meinen Freund".

example 3:

Ich schicke **meinem** Freund einen Brief. (I send a letter to my boyfriend.)

- gender of "Freund": male
- numerus of "Freund": singular
- case of "Freund" here: dative ("Ich" is the subject. "Brief" is the direct object of the sentence. "Freund" is the indirect object of the sentence => dative)

If you look for singular, male, dative you'll find the ending "em". So it must be "meinem Freund".

"Declension" of the possessive pronoun: **mein** (=my)

case	singular			plural
	male	female	neuter	-
Nominativ	mein Mann	meine Frau	mein Keind	meine Keinder
Genitiv	meines Mannes	meiner Frau	meines Keindes	meiner Keinder
Dativ	meinem Mann	meiner Frau	meinem Keind	meinen Keindern
Akkusativ	meinen Mann	meine Frau	mein Keind	meine Keinder

"Declension" of the possessive pronoun: **dein** (=your, singular)

case	singular			plural
	male	female	neuter	-
Nominativ	dein Mann	deine Frau	dein Keind	deine Keinder
Genitiv	deines Mannes	deiner Frau	deines Keindes	deiner Keinder
Dativ	deinem Mann	deiner Frau	deinem Keind	deinen Keindern
Akkusativ	deinen Mann	deine Frau	dein Keind	deine Keinder

"Declension" of the possessive pronoun: sein (=his, its)

case	singular			plural
	male	female	neuter	-
Nominativ	sein Mann	seine Frau	sein Keind	seine Keinder
Genitiv	seines Mannes	seiner Frau	seines Keindes	seiner Keinder
Dativ	seinem Mann	seiner Frau	seinem Keind	seinen Keindern
Akkusativ	seinen Mann	seine Frau	sein Keind	seine Keinder

"Declension" of the possessive pronoun: ihr (=her, their)

case	singular			plural
	male	female	neuter	-
Nominativ	ihr Mann	ihre Frau	ihr Keind	ihre Keinder
Genitiv	ihres Mannes	ihrer Frau	ihres Keindes	ihrer Keinder
Dativ	ihrem Mann	ihrer Frau	ihrem Keind	ihren Keindern
Akkusativ	ihren Mann	ihre Frau	ihr Keind	ihre Keinder

"Declension" of the possessive pronoun: unser (=our)

case	singular			plural
	male	female	neuter	-
Nominativ	unser Vater	unsere Mutter	unser Keind	unsere Keinder
Genitiv	unseres Vaters	unserer Mutter	unseres Keindes	unserer Keinder
Dativ	unserem Vater	unserer Mutter	unserem Keind	unseren Keindern
Akkusativ	unseren Vater	unsere Mutter	unser Keind	unsere Keinder

Declension" of the possessive pronoun: **euer** (=your, plural)

case	singular			plural
	male	female	neuter	-
case	singular	plural		
	male	female	neuter	-
Nominativ	unser Vater	unsere Mutter	unser Keind	unsere Keinder
Genitiv	unseres Vaters	unserer Mutter	unseres Keindes	unserer Keinder

As you can see all the possessive pronouns have got the same endings. So, you have to learn just one and you know all. If you compare it with the "declension" of indefinite articles you will see they also have the same endings. That makes it much easier.

ss

Of course there is an exception. The possessive pronoun "euer" (=your, plural) drops the "e" in the middle (marked with a *) if it has got an ending.

Unterschied zw. Possessivpronomen und Possessivartikeln

- *„Wem gehört der Ball?" – „Das ist **mein** Ball."*
- Possessivartikel, weil das Nomen dahinter steht.
- *„Wem gehört der Ball?" – „Das ist **meiner**."*

⇒ Possessivpronomen, da **kein** Nomen dahinter steht.

Pronomen ersetzen Nomen. Das bedeutet, dass es mit einem Nomen dahinter ein Possessivartikel (also ein Begleiter) ist und nur alleinstehend, also ohne Nomen, es ein Possessivpronomen ist. Der Unterschied ist wichtig, da die Deklination im Nominativ und Akkusativ unterschiedlich ist.

	meinem	Meinem	meiner	Meine- n
Dativ	meinem	Meinem	meiner	Meine- n
Akkusativ	meinen	Mein	meine	

Spätestens jetzt solltest du das System dahinter erkennen! Du musst nur wissen
Was sind Possessivartikel?
Possessivartikel stehen vor dem Nomen.
Sie geben an, wem etwas gehört und zeigen somit den Besitz oder Zugehörigkit an.
Beispiel:
- *„Das ist Anna. **Ihre** Katze spielt im Garten.“*

Possessivartikel - Formen

Die Form des Possessivartikels richtet sich nach der Person, auf die es sich bezieht:
- *„**Mein** Opa ist 80 Jahre alt. **Sein** Bruder ist 75 Jahre alt.“*
- *„Wie alt ist **dein** Opa?“*

Die **Bezugsperson** zeigt das Possessiv an, **nicht den Kasus, Genus und Numerus.**
Die Deklination wird durch das Nomen hinter dem Possessivartikel bestimmt.

Deklination der PossessivartikelPossessivartikel müssen genauso wie jeder andere Artikel dekliniert werden:

Die Deklination ist für alle Possessivartikel gleich (meinem, deinem, seinem, ihrem, unserem,...).**Ausnahme:**
euer Vater ⇒ eu**r**en Vater

Sobald eine Endung an "euer" angehangen wird, entfällt das "e" in der Mitte.

Analyse eines Beispiels:

Die Bezugsperson ist Anna. ⇒ **Possessiv:** 3. Person Weiblich ⇒ ihr

„Katze" ist das Nomen, zu dem der Artikel gehört.

⇒ <u>Numerus</u>: Singular (nur eine Katze)

⇒ **Genus:** Weiblich (<u>die</u> Katze)

⇒ **Fall (Kasus):** Nominativ

⇒ Nominativ + Singular + Weiblich = ihre

Weitere Beispiele:

A: *„Das ist Jens. **Sein** Auto steht vor **unserem** Haus.“*

B: *„Ist Jens **dein** Freund?“*

A: *„Ja, Jens ist **mein** Freund. Er holt mich ab.“*
B: *„Na dann viel Spaß bei **eurem** Ausflug.“*
A: *„Danke, werden wir haben."*

	maskulin (der)	Neutrum (das)	feminin (die)	Plural	Meaning
Ich	mein	mein	meine	meine	my
Du	dein	dein	deine	deine	your
er	sein	sein	seine	seine	his
es	sein	sein	seine	seine	its
Sie	ihr	ihr	ihre	ihre	her
Wir	Unser	Unser	Unsere	Unsere	our
ihr	euer	euer	euere	euere	your
sie	ihr	ihr	ihre	ihre	their
Sie	Ihr	Ihr	Ihre	Ihre	Your - formal

Meaning					Meaning
your	maskulin (der)	Neutrum (das)	feminin (die)	Plural	your
Nominativ	dein	dein	deine	deine	Nominativ
Akkusativ	deinem	dein	deine	deine	Akkusativ
Dativ	deinem	deinem	deiner	deinen -n	Dativ
Genetiv	deines -s/ -es	deines -s/ -es	deiner	deiner	Genetiv

Meaning				
His	maskulin (der)	Neutrum (das)	feminin (die)	Plural
Nominativ	sein	sein	seine	seine
Akkusativ	seinem	sein	seine	seine
Dativ	seinem	seinem	seiner	seinen -n
Genetiv	seines -s/ -es	seines -s/ -es	seiner	seiner

Meaning				
Her	maskulin (der)	Neutrum (das)	feminin (die)	Plural
Nominativ	ihr	ihr	ihre	ihre
Akkusativ	ihrem	ihr	ihre	ihre
Dativ	ihrem	ihrem	ihrer	ihren -n
Genetiv	ihres -s/ -es	ihres -s/ -es	ihrer	ihrer

Meaning				
Our	maskulin (der)	Neutrum (das)	feminin (die)	Plural
Nominativ	unser	unser	unsere	unsere
Akkusativ	unserem	unser	unsere	unsere
Dativ	unserem	unserem	unserer	unseren -n
Genetiv	unseres -s/ -es	unseres -s/ -es	unserer	unserer

Meaning				
Your	maskulin (der)	Neutrum (das)	feminin (die)	Plural
Nominativ	unser	unser	unsere	unsere
Akkusativ	unserem	unser	unsere	unsere
Dativ	unserem	unserem	unserer	unseren -n
Genetiv	unseres -s/ -es	unseres -s/ -es	unserer	unserer

Meaning				
Your	maskulin (der)	Neutrum (das)	feminin (die)	Plural
Nominativ	euer	euer	euere	euere
Akkusativ	euerem	euer	euere	euere
Dativ	euerem	euerem	euerer	eueren -n
Genetiv	eueres -s/ -es	eueres -s/ -es	euerer	euerer

Meaning				
	maskulin (der)	Neutrum (das)	feminin (die)	Plural
Nominativ	ihr	ihr	ihre	ihre
Akkusativ	ihrem	ihr	ihre	ihre
Dativ	ihrem	ihrem	ihrer	ihren -n
Genetiv	ihres -s/ -es	ihres -s/ -es	ihrer	ihrer

Meaning				
	maskulin (der)	Neutrum (das)	feminin (die)	Plural
Nominativ	ihr	ihr	ihre	ihre
Akkusativ	ihrem	ihr	ihre	ihre
Dativ	ihrem	ihrem	ihrer	ihren -n
Genetiv	ihres -s/ -es	ihres -s/ -es	ihrer	ihrer

Meaning				
	maskulin (der)	Neutrum (das)	feminin (die)	Plural
Nominativ	ihr	ihr	ihre	ihre
Akkusativ	ihrem	ihr	ihre	ihre
Dativ	ihrem	ihrem	ihrer	ihren -n
Genetiv	ihres -s/ -es	ihres -s/ -es	ihrer	ihrer

Meaning				
	maskulin (der)	**Neutrum (das)**	**feminin (die)**	**Plural**
Nominativ	**ihr**	**ihr**	**ihre**	**ihre**
Akkusativ	**ihrem**	**ihr**	**ihre**	**ihre**
Dativ	**ihrem**	**ihrem**	**ihrer**	**ihren -n**
Genetiv	**ihres -s/ -es**	**ihres -s/ -es**	**ihrer**	**ihrer**

Meaning				
	maskulin (der)	Neutrum (das)	feminin (die)	Plural
Nominativ	dieser	diese	diese	diese
Akkusativ	diesen	dieses	diese	diese
Dativ	diesem	diesem	dieser	diesen -n
Genetiv	dieses -s /es	dieses -s /es	dieser	dieser

Possessivpronomen I (Übersicht)			
	Singular	Plural	
1. Person	mein (ich)	unser (wir)	
2. Person	dein (du)	euer (ihr)	
	Ihr (Sie)	Ihr (Sie)	(Höflichkitsform)
3. Person	sein (er)	ihr (sie)	
	ihr (sie)		
	sein (es)		

Possessivpronomen II (Deklination)			
Singular	maskulin (der)	feminin (die)	Neutrum (das)
Nominativ	mein	meine	mein
Genitiv	meines	meiner	meines
Dativ	meinem	meiner	meinem
Akkusativ	meinen	meine	mein

Possessivpronomen III (Deklination)			
Plural			
	maskulin (der)	feminin (die)	Neutrum (das)
Nominativ	meine	meine	meine
Genitiv	meiner	meiner	meiner
Dativ	meinen	meinen	meinen
Akkusativ	meine	meine	meine

Bildung

1. Die Person (ich, du, er, sie, es, wir, ihr, sie, Sie) wird durch den Besitzer bestimmt.

2. Die Endung wird durch den Genus des Nomens, auf das es sich bezieht, bestimmt.

3. Der Fall wird durch die Situation im Satz, in dem das Personalpronomen steht, bestimmt.

„Wem gehört der Ball?" (Genus = maskulin)

Person	Basisform	Pronomen	Fall
ich	mein	→ „Das ist meiner!"	
du	dein	→ „Das ist deiner!"	
er	sein	→ „Das ist seiner!"	
sie	ihr	→ „Das ist ihrer!"	→ Nominativ
es	sein	→ „Das ist seiner!"	→ Maskulin = „der"
wir	unser	→ „Das ist unserer!"	→ Endung „er"
ihr	euer	→ „Das ist eurer!"	
sie/Sie	Ihr/Ihr	→ „Das ist ihrer/Ihrer!"	

Deklination der Possessivpronomen

Die Deklination unterscheidet sich nur im Nominativ (Maskulin + Neutral) und im Akkusativ (Neutral) von der Deklination der Possessivartikel.

Die Possessivpronomen bekommen immer die Endung des bestimmten Artikels. Auch im Nominativ (m/n) und im Akkusativ (n).

	Genus	Nominativ	Akkusativ	Dativ	Genitiv
Singular	Maskulin	meiner	meinen	meinem	meines
	Neutral	meins	**meins**	meinem	meines
	Feminin	meine	meine	meiner	meiner
Plural		meine	meine	meinen	meiner

Anhand der Endungen kannst du erkennen, dass die Endungen exakt denen der bestimmten Artikel entsprechen.

	male	female	neutral	plural
Nominative	mein	meine	mein	meine
Accusative	meinen	meine	mein	meine
Dative	meinem	meiner	meinem	meinen ...n
Genitive	meines ...s	meiner	meines ...s	meiner

Masculine	Feminine	Neuter	Plural
meinen	meine	mein	meine
deinen	deine	dein	deine
seinen	seine	sein	seine
ihren	ihre	ihr	ihre
seinen	seine	sein	seine
unseren	unsere	unser	unsere
euren	eure	euer	eure
ihren	ihre	ihr	ihre
Ihren	Ihre	Ihr	Ihre

Tips and tricks
Maskuline Nomen (der):

Merkmal	Beispiele
Männliche Personen	der Mann, der Student, der Vater, ...
Berufe	der Architekt, der Arzt, der Mechaniker, ...
Himmelsrichtungen	der Westen, der Osten, der Norden, ...
Tage, Monate, Jahreszeiten	der Montag, der März, der Winter, ...
Fast alle Flüsse außerhalb Deutschlands	der Nil, der Amazonas, der Ganges, ...
Fast alle Berge	der Kilimandscharo, der Mt. Everest, der Vesuv, ...
Niederschlag	der Regen, der Schnee, der Hagel, ...
Nomen mit der Endung: -ling	der Liebling, der Schmetterling, der Lehrling, ...
Nomen mit der Endung: -ismus	der Kommunismus, der Kapitalismus, der Hinduismus, ...
Nomen mit der Endung: -ich	der Teppich, der Kranich, der Deich, ...

Further endings, which mostly indicate a masculine noun: -ig, -ent, -ier, -ist, -or, -ör, -iker, -ast, -eur.
These traits can help you, but you should ALWAYS learn the meaning of the word along with the article (gender).

Maskuline Artikel Merkmale

Weitere Endungen, die meistens ein maskulines Nomen anzeigen: -ig, -ent, -ier, -ist, -or, -ör, -iker, -ast, -eur.

Diese Merkmale können dir helfen, aber du solltest die Bedeutung des Wortes IMMER zusammen mit dem Artikel (Genus) lernen.

Feminine Nomen (die):
Feminine Nomen Merkmale

Weitere Endungen, die meistens ein feminines Nomen anzeigen: -anz, -ik, -tät, -ur, -ei, -sis, -ive, -ade.

Neutrale Nomen (das):
Neutrale Nomen Merkmale
Weitere Endungen, die meistens ein neutrales Nomen anzeigen: -tel, -in, -tum, -um, -o, -ma, -ett,

Zusammengesetzte Nomen
Besteht ein Nomen aus mehr als einem Teil-Nomen, bestimmt immer das letzte

Nomen das Genus des gesamten Wortes.

Beispiele:
- der Schrank + die Tür = die Schranktür
- das Bett + die Decke = die Bettdecke
- die Hand + das Tuch = das Handtuch

Empfehlung: Sind das zu viele **Reg**eln für dich? Dann melde dich jetzt für meinen kostenlosen Grammatikkurs an. In der ersten Lektion zeige ich dir, wie du OHNE WÖRTERBUCH 75% aller Artikel richtig rätst! Jetzt anmelden!
Die gute Nachricht
Im Plural sind alle Nomen gleich, e.gal ob maskulin, feminin oder neutral:
„der Ball" ⇒ „die Bälle"
„die Frau" ⇒ „die Frauen"
„das Haus" ⇒ „die Häuser" Verb Conjugation - Present-Past-Perfect

Subjunctive
Introduction
We can use the subjunctive mood, Konjunktiv in German, to expreß unreal situations such as wishes, hypothetical situations and unreal conditional clauses, or to repeating what people say in indirect speech. Click on one of the links below for a detailed online leßon. There are exercises at the end of each page so you can put your knowledge to the test.

Subjunctive I (Konjunktiv I)
Subjunctive I (Konjunktiv I) is generally used in newspaper articles and reports and when statements are repeated as indirect or reported speech. It is also used in some idiomatic expressions.
Example:
Er sagte, es sei bekannt, dass er viel arbeite.

Subjunctive II (Konjunktiv II)
Subjunctive II (Konjunktiv II) expresses imaginary, unrealistic or hypothetical situations. We can also use the it in indirect speech or for polite questions/statements.
Example:
Ich wünschte, ich hätte mehr Zeit.

The conjugation in the subjunctive I and II and in the present tense, past tense, perfect, pluperfect and future tense for the verb fragen (Irregular)

Present Subject.

Present		Imperfect		Perfect		
ich	frage	ich	frug	ich	habe	gefragt
du	fragest	du	frugst	du	hast	gefragt
er	frage	er	frug	er	hat	gefragt
wir	fragen	wir	frugen	wir	haben	gefragt
ihr	fraget	ihr	frugt	ihr	habt	gefragt
sie	fragen	sie	frugen	sie	haben	gefragt

Konjunktiv I – Special Subjunctive in German

The special subjunctive, also called subjunctive 1 or present subjunctive (Konjunktiv I), is primarily used in newspaper articles and reports when statements are repeated as indirect speech. The special subjunctive is also used in certain idiomatic expressions.
Learn the rules for conjugating the present subjunctive in German grammar and get tips on when to use it. Then put your knowledge to the test in the exercises.

Example

Hoch lebe das Geburtstagskeind! Zu seinem 90. Geburtstag sagte der Schauspieler, er habe sich noch nie so jung gefühlt.

Usage
The subjunctiv I is used to express:
indirect speech (in colloquial speech the indicative is more common; see indirect speech)
Example:
Er sagt, er habe sich noch nie so jung gefühlt.

Some Idiomatik Expression
Example:

Hoch lebe das Geburtstagskeind!
Conjugation of German Verbs in Subjunctive I
There are a few points to consider when conjugating the subjunctive I:
Only the verb sein is still common in all its subjunctive I forms:
ich sei, du sei(e)st, er sei, wir seien, ihr seiet, sie seien

Example:
Er sagte, sie seien im Keino.

We generally only use the subjunctive I in the 3rd person singular (er/sie/es/man) with all other verbs. We only have to remove the n from the infinitive.
Example:
haben – er habe
schreiben – er schreibe

In the 2nd person (du/ihr), the only difference between the subjunctive I and the indicative is that there is an e before the ending in the subjunctive form.
Example:
Du träumst – du träumest
ihr geht – ihr gehet

It is common to use the subjunctive II in the second person, instead of the subjunctive I because it's easier to tell it apart from the indicative.
There is no difference between the subjunctive I and the indicative in the 1st person singular (ich), as well as the 1st and 3rd person plural (wir, sie) which is why we have to use the subjunctive II in this situation.
Example:
„Sie gehen joggen." – Er sagt, sie gingen joggen. (subj. II)

Tenses in the Subjunctive I

We can use the subjunctive I in the present, present perfect, and future tenses.

present	er gehe
present perfect	er sei ge.gangen
future	er werde gehen
future perfect	er werde ge.gangen sein

Konjunktiv II – The General Subjunctive in German

The general subjunctive, also: past subjunctive or subjunctive 2 (Konjunktiv II), expresses hypothetical situations. It is also used in indirect speech and in polite questions and statements.
Learn how to conjugate subjunctive II in German grammar and get tips on how and when to use it. In the exercises, you can practise what you have learnt.

Example
Usage :   We use the German subjunctive II (Konjunktiv II) for:
Unreal or hypothetical wishes and hopes
Example: Ich wünschte, ich hätte Ferien.

Unreal statements and conditional clauses (see conditional clauses)
Example: Dann könnte ich in den Urlaub fahren.
Wenn ich im Urlaub wäre, läge ich den ganzen Tag am Strand.

Indirect speech when the subjunctive I can't be used (see also indirect speech)
Example: Unser Lehrer sagt, wir müßten noch viel lernen.

Polite or tentative questions or statements
Example: Wärst du so freundlich, an die Tafel zu kommen?
Conjugation of German Verbs in Subjunctive II

There are two forms of the subjunctive II, one expresses situations in the present and the other situations in the past.

Situations in the Present
To express situations in the present with the general subjunctive:
We add the subjunctive ending to the simple past stem (see table below, in the column finden). Strong verbs get an Umlaut.
Example: finden (fand) – er fände

Weak verbs and some mixed verbs look the same in the subjunctive II as they do in the indicative simple past. Because of this, we generally use würde with these verbs (würde form).
Example: ich wartete – ich würde warten

In spoken German, the würde + infinitive is prefered for many strong verbs.
Example: gehen – ich ginge/ich würde gehen

1st person singular	ich fände	ich wäre	ich hätte	ich würde ...
2nd person singular	du fändest	du wär(e)st	du hättest	du würdest ...
3rd person singular	er fände	er wäre	er hätte	er würde ...
1st person singular	ich fände	ich wäre	ich hätte	ich würde ...
2nd person singular	du fändest	du wär(e)st	du hättest	du würdest ...
3rd person singular	er fände	er wäre	er hätte	er würde ...

1st person singular	ich fände	ich wäre	ich hätte	ich würde ...
2nd person singular	du fändest	du wär(e)st	du hättest	du würdest ...
3rd person singular	er fände	er wäre	er hätte	er würde ...

1st Person plural	wir fänden	wir wären	wir hätten	wir würden ...
2nd Person plural	ihr fändet	ihr wär(e)t	ihr hättet	ihr würdet ...
3rd Person plural	sie fänden	sie wären	sie hätten	sie würden ...

Situations in the Past
If we want to express a situation in the past, we use the subjunctive forms of sein/haben + past participle.

Example: ich wäre ge.gangen/ich hätte gesagt.

Verb conjugation
A verb is word which shows action or position.
The original form of a verb is called the "Infinitive form"
This infinitive form is conjugated as per the subject of the sentence and is called conjugated form
The conjugation depends on the number and person.
In some languages, gender also plays a role but not in German.
A verb is word which shows action or position.
The original form of a verb is called the "infinitive form"
This infinitive form is conjugated as per the subject of the sentence and is called conjugated form
The conjugation depends on the number and person.
In some languages, gender also plays a role but not in German.

1	Regular (exactly according to the rules) (more than 80% fall under this)	
2	e' changes into "I"/"ie", but only with Du, er/es/sie	
3	"a" changes into " ae", , but only with Du, er/es/sie	
4	**Irregular** (no concrete or exact rule)	

Two things must be noted:

a	Sein is a complete exception. It does not follow any rule. It has its own conjugation.
b	Changes do occur in second, third and fourth category, but it occurs only with Du and er/es/sie and sometimes with ich in the **Irregular** category. Conjugation of plural never ever changes and it remains the same rule for all the four categories.

How to conjugate

1. Remove -en
2. Put the endings according to the rules
3. With Du, Er/ es/ sie and ihr there are two endings. After removing en from the verb, if the verb ends with -d or -t, put an extra -e E.g. Finden, arbeiten, antworten etc.
4. Those verbs which end with -s, -ß, Beta, -tz after removing -en, they take only -t ending Du E.g. Lese, sitzen, heiße, essen, vergessen

Use and conjugation of Trennbar (Separable) verbs :
There are some verbs which are separable ie, it can be separated into two parts. First part goes at the end of the sentence and second part is conjugated according to the subject.
Usually the second part if the verb which is conjugated is an independent verb also. But both the different meanings - a word as an independent verb and as a part of the Trennbar (separable) verb.
E.g. machen - to do
aufmachen - to open
The conjugation of the Trennbar (Separable) verbs are done as per the rules of conjugation. The only change while conjugating is that the first part is written at the end.
Some examples are given on the page of conjugation
Use - Ich rufe meine Freundin an.
Er lädt seinen Onkel ein.
If a Trennbar (Separable) verb comes with a "Modal" verb or "werden", Modal verb comes at the 2nd place and the Trennbar (Separable) verb goes to the end of the sentence in its infinitive form and without being Separated.
E.g. Ich will meine Freundin anrufen
Er soll seinen Onkel einladen
If a Trennbar (Separable) verb comes with a sub-ordinating conjunction (Wenn, weil, wie, ob, obwohl, dass, ab), in which the verb goes at end, the Trennbar (Separable) in its Conjugated Form and without being separated.
E.g. Ich habe **keine** Zeit, weil ich mein Zimmer aufraeume.
In a Satzfrage, the second part of the verb comes at first place in its conjugated form and the first part goes to end.
In case of "Modal" verb, the "Modal" verb will come at first place in its conjugated form and the Trennbar (Separable) verb will come at the end in its inifinitive form.
E.g. Rufst Du deinen Freund and
Willst Du deinen Freund anrufen?

Use and Conjugation of Modal Verbs:
If there is a Modal verb in a sentence, the Modal verb comes at 2nd place in its conjugated form and the main verb goes at the end of the sentence in its infinitive form ie. the main verb is not conjugated.
E.g. Er soll jetzt schlafen
Er soll gehen

Ich will essen

There are seven Modal Verbs
Wollen -to want, wish, desire
Sollen - Should
Koennen - Could, can , be able to
Dürfen - may, be allowed to
Moegen - to like
Müßen - must, have to
moecheten - would like to
(Conjugation- is defined as per conjugation of **Irregular** or strong Verbs)

Verb Conjugation (I) Regular

	Ich	Du	Er/es/sie	Wir	ihr	sie/ Sie
spielen	spiele	spielst	spielt	spielen	spielt	spielen
kommen	komme	kommst	kommt	kommen	kommt	kommen
gehen	gehe	gehst	geht	gehen	geht	gehen
wohnen	wohne	wohnst	wohnt	wohnen	wohnt	wohnen
sagen	sage	sagst	sagt	sagen	sagt	sagen
bekommen	bekomme	bekommst	bekommt	bekommen	bekommt	bekommen
finden	finde	findest	findet	finden	findet	finden
arbeiten	arbeite	arbeitest	arbeitet	arbeiten	arbeitet	arbeiten
antworten	antworte	antwortest	antwortet	antworten	antwortet	antworten
hängen	hänge	hängst	hängt	hängen	hängt	hängen
stellen	stelle	stellst	stellt	stellen	stellt	stellen
entschuldigen	entschuldige	entschuldigst	entschuldigt	entschuldigen	entschuldigt	entschuldigen
stehen	stehe	stehst	steht	stehen	steht	stehen
legen	le.ge	le.gst	le.gt	legen	le.gt	legen
liegen	liege	liegst	liegt	liegen	liegt	liegen
schreiben	schreibe	schreibst	schreibt	schreiben	schreibt	schreiben
bringen	bringe	bringst	bringt	bringen	brigt	bringen
mitbringen	mitbringe	mitbringst	mitbringt	mitbringen	mitbringt	mitbringen

Verb Conjugation (2) (e - i/ie)

	ich	du	er/es/sie	wir	ihr	sie/ sie
helfen	helfe	hilfst	hilft	helfen	helft	helfen
geben	geb(e)	gibst	gibt	geben	gebt	geben
sprechen	sprech(e)	sprichst	spricht	sprechen	sprecht	sprechen
werfen	werf(e)	wirfst	wirft	werfen	werft	werfen
nehmen	nehm(e)	nimmst	nimmt	nehmen	nehmt	nehmen
mitnehmen	nehm(e) mit	nimmst mit	nimmt mit	nehmen mit	nehmt mit	nehmen mit
essen	ess(e)	isst	isst	essen	esst	essen
vergessen	vergess(e)	vergisst	vergisst	vergessen	vergesst	vergessen
brechen	brech(e)	brichst	bricht	brechen	brecht	brechen
lesen	les(e)	liest	liest	lesen	lest	lesen
sehen	seh(e)	siehst	sieht	sehen	seht	sehen
treffen	treff(e)	triffst	trifft	treffen	trefft	treffen
fressen	fress(e)	frisst	frisst	fressen	fresst	fressen
stehen	steh(e)	stehst	steht	stehen	steht	stehen
gelten	gelt(e)	giltst	gilt	gelten	geltet	gelten
treten	tret(e)	trittst	tritt	treten	tretet	treten
aussehen	seh(e) aus	siehst aus	ieht aus	seh(e)n aus	seht aus	seh(e)n aus
eintreten	tret(e) ein	trittst ein	tritt ein	treten ein	tretet ein	treten ein

Verb Conjugation (3) (-a -ae)

	ich	du	er/es/sie	wir	ihr	sie/ sie
fahren	fahr(e)	fährst	fährt	fahren	fahrt	fahren
laufen	lauf(e)	läufst	läuft	laufen	lauft	laufen
fallen	fall(e)	fällst	fällt	fallen	fallt	fallen
schlafen	schlaf(e)	schläfst	schläft	schlafen	schlaft	schlafen
schlagen	schlag(e)	schlägst	schlägt	schlagen	schlagt	schlagen
abfahren	fahr(e) ab	fährst ab	fährt ab	fahren ab	fahrt ab	fahren ab
waschen	wasch(e)	wäsch(s) t	wäscht	waschen	wascht	waschen
tragen	trag(e)	trägst	trägt	tragen	tragt	tragen
laden	lad(e)	lädst	lädt	laden	ladet	laden
halten	halt(e)[s]	hältst	hält	halten	haltet	halten
fangen	fang(e)	fängst	fängt	fangen	fangt	fangen
anfangen	fang(e) an	fängst an	fängt an	fangen an	fangt an	fangen an
braten	brat(e)	brätst	brät	braten	bratet	braten

Verb Conjugation (3) (-a -ae)

	ich	du	er/es/sie	wir	ihr	sie/ sie
sein	bin	bist	ist	sind	seid	sind
haben	hab(e)	hast	hat	haben	habt	haben
werden	werd(e)	wirst	wird	werden	werdet	werden
wollen	will	willst	will	wollen	wollt	wollen
sollen	soll	sollst	soll	sollen	sollt	sollen
können	kann	kannst	kann	können	könnt	können
dürfen	darf	darfst	darf	dürfen	dürft	dürfen
müssen	muss	musst	muss	müssen	müsst	müssen
mögen	mag	magst	mag	mögen	mögt	mögen
möchten	möcht(e)	möchtest	möchte	möchten	möchtet	möchten
wissen	weiß	weißt	weiß	wissen	wisst	wissen
tun	tu(e)	tust	tut	tun	tut	tun
sammeln	samm(e)l(e)	sammelst	sammelt	sammeln	sammelt	sammeln
laden	lad(e)	lädst	lädt	laden	ladet	laden
einladen	lad(e)[5] ein	lädst ein	lädt ein	laden ein	ladet ein	laden ein

Verb -Past tense (Praeteritum)

There are two types of verbs
1. **Regular or weak**
2. **Irregular or Strong**

Regular or weak verbs have a fixed or definite rule for forming past tense while **Irregular** verbs have no such fixed rule.
Conjugation of Ich, er/es /Sie remains same in past tense
Only the conjugated form with er/es/Sie is said and not the infinitive form of the verb in past tense. E.G.
Spielen - spielte / komen - kam
The rules of conjugation remain the same as of present tense. The Endings are same except with Er/Es/Sie. Which do not take -t / - te as ending and have the same form as of "ich". In Strong Verbs, even, "Ich" does not take any ending.

The rules of usage are exactly the same.

	Ich	Du	Er/es/sie	Wir	ihr	sie/ Sie
fragen	fragte	fragtest	fragte	fragten	fragtet	fragten
antworte	antwortete	antwortetest	antwortete	antworteten	antwortetet	antworteten
kommen	kam	kamst	kam	kamen	kamt	kamen
gehen	ging	gingst	ging	gingen	gingt	gingen
an kommen	kam an	kamst an	kam an	kamen an	kamt an	kamen an

Past of **Regular** or weak verbs

a		How to make past form of a Regular verb
1		**Remove -en**
2		**Add -t / -et (If the verb ends with -d / -t, then use -et, otherwise -t)**
3		**Put the ending -e, which is also the conjugation of**

Ich, Er/Es/ Sie

e.g.   **spielen - spiel -spielt - spielte Or**
       arbeiten - arbeit - arbeitet - arbeitete

b   **Past of Irregular or / Strong Verbs**

There is no fixed rule, One needs to learn it. However, there are some Clue(s)s, which make it very easy to learn. Strong verbs do not take -e as ending with Ich, Er/ Es/ Sie. E.g. Kommen - kam, fahren - fuhr, ankommen - kam.. An, abfahren - fuhr..ab

Clue(s)s :

a   These verbs, in which "e" changes into "I" or "ie" in the conjugation in present tense, "e" changes into "a" in past tense e.g. Helfen - half, geben- gab, lesen - las, sehen -sah etc.

b   "ei" changes into "ie",. E.g. Bleiben - blieb, Schreiben -schrieb, laufen - lief,

c.   "I" changes into "a", E.g. Beginen - Begna, schwimmen- schwamm etc.

d.   "ie" change into "o", E.g filegen - flog, bieten -bot etc

e.   Exception - which take "e" as ending the same way as weak verb.
       e.g. Haben- hatten, bringen - brachten, denken - dachten

f.   Must learn where there are no Clue(s)s.
       E.g. Sein -war, gehen -ging, kommen – kam

g.   The rules of conjugation remain same as of Present Tense. The endings are same except with er/es/sie. Which do not take - t or -et as endings and have the same form as that of Ich in strong verbs, even „Ich" does not take any ending
The rule of usage are exactly the same.

Verb - Past tense - **Regular (weak) Verbs**

	ich	du	er/es/sie	wir	ihr	sie/ sie
Arbeiten	arbeitete	arbeitetest	arbeitete	arbeiteten	arbeitetet	arbeiteten
Aufmachen	machte auf	machtest auf	machte auf	machten auf	machtet auf	machten auf
Besuchen	besuchtest	besuchtest	besuchte	besuchten	besuchtet	besuchten
Bezahlen	bezahlte	bezahltest	bezahlte	bezahlten	bezahltet	bezahlten
brauchen	brauchte	brauchtest	brauchte	brauchten	brauchtet	brauchten
denken	dachte	dachtest	dachte	dachten	dachtet	dachten
einkaufen	kaufte ein	kauftest ein	kaufte ein	kauften ein	kauftet ein	kauften ein
fragen	fragte	fragtest	fragte	fragten	fragtet	fragten
gehören	gehörte	gehörtest	gehörte	gehörten	gehörtet	gehörten
glauben	glaubte	glaubtest	glaubte	glaubten	glaubtet	glaubten
hängen	hing	hingst	hing	hingen	hingt	hingen
hassen	hasste	hasstest	hasste	hassten	hasstet	hassten
heiraten	heiratete	heiratetest	heiratete	heirateten	heiratetet	heirateten
hören	hörte	hörtest	hörte	hörten	hörtet	hörten
kaufen	kaufte	kauftest	kaufte	kauften	kauftet	kauften
kennen	kannte	kanntest	kannte	kannten	kanntet	kannten
klopfen	klopfte	klopftest	klopfte	klopften	klopftet	klopften
legen	le.gte	le.gtest	le.gte	le.gten	le.gtet	le.gten
lieben	liebte	liebtest	liebte	liebten	liebtet	liebten
lernen	lernte	lerntest	lernte	lernten	lerntet	lernten
machen	machte	machtest	machte	machten	machtet	machten
sagen	sagte	sagtest	sagte	sagten	sagtet	sagten
schenken	schenkte	schenktest	schenkte	schenkten	schenktet	schenkten
schicken	schickte	schicktest	schickte	schickten	schicktet	schickten
setzen	setzte	setztest	setzte	setzten	setztet	setzten
spielen	spielte	spieltest	spielte	spielten	spieltet	spielten
stecken	steckte	stecktest	steckte	steckten	stecktet	steckten
stellen	stellte	stelltest	stellte	stellten	stelltet	stellten
stören	störte	störtest	störte	störten	störtet	störten
suchen	suchte	suchtest	suchte	suchten	suchtet	suchten
tanzen	tanzte	tanztest	tanzte	tanzten	tanztet	tanzten
verkaufen	verkaufte	verkauftest	verkaufte	verkauften	verkauftet	verkauften
versuchen	versuchte	versuchtest	versuchte	versuchten	versuchtet	versuchten

warten	wartete	wartetest	wartete	warteten	wartetet	warteten
weinen	weinte	weintest	weinte	weinten	weintet	weinten
wiederholen	wiederholte	wiederholtest	wiederholte	wiederholten	wiederholtet	wiederholten
wohnen	wohnte	wohntest	wohnte	wohnten	wohntet	wohnten
zumachen	machte zu	machtest zu	machte zu	machten zu	machtet zu	machten zu
frühstücken	frühstückte	frühstücktest	frühstückte	frühstückten	frühstücktet	frühstückten
antworten	antwortete	antwortetest	antwortete	antworteten	antwortetet	antwortete

Verb - Past tense - **Irregular** (Strong) Verbs

	Ich	Du	Er/es/sie	Wir	ihr	sie/ Sie
aussteigen	stieg	stiegst	stieg	stiegen	stiegt	stiegen
backen	buk	bukst	buk	buken	bukt	buken
beginnen	begann	begannst	begann	begannen	begannt	begannen
bieten	bot	bot(e)[7]st	bot	boten	botet	boten
bleiben	blieb	bliebst	blieb	blieben	bliebt	blieben
brennen	brannte	branntest	brannte	brannten	branntet	brannten
denken	dachte	dachtest	dachte	dachten	dachtet	dachten
dürfen	durfte	durftest	durfte	durften	durftet	durften
einsteigen	Stieg ein	Stiegst ein	Stieg ein	Stiegen ein	Stiegt ein	Stiegen ein
Essen	aß	aß(es)t	aß	aßen	aß(e)t	Aßen
fahren	fuhr	fuhrst	fuhr	fuhren	fuhrt	fuhren
fallen	fiel	fielst	fiel	fielen	fielt	fielen
finden	fand	fand(e) st	fand	fanden	fandet	fanden
fliegen	flog	flogst	flog	flogen	flogt	flogen
fliehen	flohst	flohst	floh	floh(e)[5]n	floht	floh(e)[5]n
fressen	fraß	fraß(es)t	fraß	fraßen	fraß(e)t	fraßen
geben	gab	gabst	gab	gaben	gabt	gaben
gelten	galt	galt(e)[7]st	galt	galten	galtet	galten
genießen	genoss	genoss(es)t	genoss	genossen	genoss(e)t	genossen
gewinnen	gewann	gewannst	gewann	gewannen	gewannt	gewannen
halten	hielt	hielt(e)[7]st	hielt	hielten	hieltet	hielten
entscheiden	entschied	entschied(e)[7]st	entschied	entschieden	entschiedet	entschieden
Sich unterhalten	Unterhielt mir/mich[3]	unterhielt(e)[7]st dir/dich[3]	Unterhielt sich	Unterhielten uns	Unterhieltet euch	Unterhielten euch
verbringen	verbrachte	verbrachtest	verbrachte	verbrachten	verbrachtet	verbrachten
tragen	trug	trugst	trug	trugen	trugt	trugen
treffen	traf	trafst	traf	trafen	traft	trafen
treten	trat	trat(e)[7]st	trat	traten	tratet	traten
trinken	trank	trankst	trank	tranken	trankt	tranken
tun	tat	tat(e)[7]st	tat	taten	tatet	taten
reiten	ritt	ritt(e)[7]st	ritt	ritten	rittet	ritten
schneiden	schnitt	schnitt(e)[7]st	schnitt	schnitten	schnittet	schnitten
heißen	hieß	hieß(es)t	hieß	hießen	hieß(e)t	hießen
liegen	lag	lagst	lag	lagen	lagt	lagen
sitzen	saß	saß(es)t	saß	saßen	saß(e)t	saßen
hängen	hing	hingst	hing	hingen	hingt	hingen
verstehen	verstand	verstand(e)[7]st	verstand	verstanden	verstandet	verstanden
fangen	fing	fingst	fing	fingen	fingt	fingen
anfangen	Fing an	Fingst an	Fing an	Fingen an	Fingt an	Fingen an
aufstehen	Stand auf	stand(e)[7]st auf	Stand auf	Standen auf	Standet auf	Standen auf
anrufen	Rief an	Riefst an	Rief an	Riefen an	Rieft an	Riefen an
ringen	rang	rangst	rang	rangen	rangt	rangen
rufen	rief	riefst	rief	riefen	rieft	riefen
schlafen	schlief	schliefst	schlief	schliefen	schlieft	schliefen
schlagen						
Schließen						
schreiben						
schwimmen						
sehen						
senden						
singen						
sollen						
sprechen						
springen						
steigen						
sterben						
Sich umziehen						
kommen						
ankommen						
bekommen						
gehen						

mitgehen					
abfahren					
stehen					
werden					
mögen					
ziehen					
einziehen					
helfen					
kennen					
klingeln					
können					
laden					
lassen					
laufen					
lesen					
müssen					
nehmen					
nennen					
raten					
rennen					
umsteigen					
vergessen					
waschen					
werfen					
wissen					
wollen					
sein					
haben					
werden					
mögen					
ziehen					
einziehen					
ausziehen					

There are two types of verbs

Regular or weak
Irregular or Strong
Regular or weak verbs have a fixed or definite rule for forming perfect tense while **Irregular** verbs have no such fixed rule.
Perfect takes helping verb with it.
German has two helping verbs
Sein
Haben
A verb has only one perfect form and comes at the end of the sentence. The helping verb "Sein" or "Haben" comes at the 2nd place and is conjugated according to the subject.

e.g.　　Der Student is gekommen.
　　　　Die Studenten sind gekommen.

Very few verbs take "Sein" as helping verb. A complete list is given in the topic "Perfect-Verbs-taking - SEIN"

1 Perfect of Regular or weak Verbs

Take "ge-" as prefix - root or stem of root the verb - "-t / et" as suffix

Verb	Prefix- ge	root	Suffix -t /et	
antworten	ge-	antwort	-et	geantwortet
arbeiten	ge-	arbeit	-et	gearbeitet
kaufen	ge-	kauf	-t	gekauft
Spielen	ge-	spiel	-t	gespielt
wohnen	ge-	wohn	-t	gewohnt

2 Perfect of Irregular or Strong Verbs

Take "ge-" as prefeix - root of the verb may not change the "-en" suffix.

Verb	Prefix- ge	root	Suffix -en	
fahren	ge-	fahr	-en	gefahren
gehen	ge-	gang	-en	ge.gangen
kommen	ge-	komm	-en	gekommen
schreiben	ge-	schrieb	-en	geschrieben

There is no fixed rule to make perfect of **Irregular** or strong verbs. There are some Clue(s)s which make it very easy to learn

1   No change in Root. e.g. kommen - gekommen, lesen -gelesen, fahren – gefahren

2   "ei" changes to "ie" e.g. bleiben - geblieben, schreiben – geschrieben

3   "i" changes to "u" , e.g. finden - gefunden, trinken – getrunken

4   "e" changes to "o", e.g. werden - geworden, treffen -getroffen, werfen -geworfen

5   "i" changes to "o", e.g. beginen - begonnen, schwimmen –
        geschwommen.

6   Exception - which take "t" as ending like weak verbs e.g. haben - gehabt, bringen - gebracht, denken
        -gedacht.

7   Must learn - where there are no Clue(s)s. e.g. sein - gewesen, verstehen - verstanden, sitzen -
        gesessen. etc.

Exceptions:

There are some verbs which do not take " ge- " as prefix.
a.   Verbs starting with "be-", "er-", "ver-", "ent-" , "ge -" (with few verbs
only) unter, über etc. E.g. Bekommen - bekommen, erklären - erklärt, verstehen - verstanden, gewinnen -
gewonnen, unterhalten - unterhalten etc.

b. Verbs ending with "ieren" E.g. Studieren - studiert, passieren - passiert etc.

c.   "-ge" comes inbetween with Trennbar (Separable) verbs. E.g. Anrufen - angerufen, einlade -
eingeladen.

Perfect - Regular or Weak Verbs

	Ich	Du	Er/es/sie	Wir	ihr	sie/ Sie
abholen						
ablehnen						
achten						
antworten						
arbeiten						
atmen						
aufmachen						
aufräumen						
ausmachen						
ausstellen						
baden						
bauen						
bedeuten						
sich beeilen						
berichten						
beschäftigen						
bestellen						
besuchen						
beten						
bezahlen						
bilden						
brauchen						

buchstabieren					
danken					
diskutieren					
einkaufen					
entschuldigen					
ergänzen					
erinnern					
erklären					
erwarten					
erzählen					
folgen					
fotografieren					
fragen					
sich freuen					
frühstücken					
fühlen					
führen					
füllen					
gehören					
glauben					
gratulieren					
hängen					
handeln					
hassen					
heiraten					
hören					
sich interessieren					
kämpfen					
kaufen					
kennenlernen					
kleben					
klopfen					
kochen					
kosten					
kühlen					
kürzen					
küssen					
lachen					
Lächeln					
leben					
legen					
leeren					
leiben					
lernen					
loben					
lösen					
machen					
malen					
meinen					
nützen					

öffnen					
organisieren					
packen					
passen					
passieren					
putzen					
reisen					
sagen					
schaden					
schauen					
schenken					
schicken					
schmerzen					
senden					
sich setzen					
sparen					
spazieren					
spielen					
stecken					
stellen					
stören					
studieren					
stürzen					
suchen					
tanzen					
telefonieren					
tele.grafieren					
träumen					
üben					
überraschen					
verdienen					
verkaufen					
verlieben					
versuchen					
vorstellen					
wählen					
wandern					
warten					
wechseln					
weinen					
wiederholen					
wohnen					
wünschen					
zahlen					
zeichnen					
zeigen					
zumachen					

List of Perfect - **Irregular** or strong Verbs

	Ich	Du	Er/es/sie	Wir	ihr	sie/ Sie
aussteigen						
backen						
Beginnen						
bieten						
bleiben						
brennen						
denke						
dürfen						
einladen						
einsteigen						
essen						
fahren						
fallen						
finden						
fliegen						
fliehen						
fressen						
geben						
gelten						
genießen						
gewinnen						
halten						
heißen						
helfen						
kennen						
klingeln						
können						
laden						
lassen						
laufen						
lesen						
müssen						
nehmen						
nennen						
raten						
rennen						
ringen						
rufen						
schlafen						
schlagen						
Schließen						
schreiben						
schwimmen						
sehen						
senden						
singen						
sollen						

sprechen						
springen						
steigen						
sterben						
tragen						
treffen						
treten						
trinken						
umsteigen						
vergessen						
waschen						
werfen						
wissen						
wollen						
sein						
haben						
werden						
mögen						
ziehen						
einziehen						
ausziehen						
umziehen						
kommen						
ankommen						
bekommen						
gehen						
mitgehen						
abfahren						
stehen						
aufstehen						
liegen						
sitzen						
hängen						
verstehen						
fangen						
anfangen						
tun						
reiten						
schneiden						
entscheiden						
unterhalten						
verbringen						
scheiden						
wehtun						
bestehen						
ausstehen						
gestehen						
gelingen						

Perfekt - Verbs taking - "SEIN"

	Ich	Du	Er/es/sie	Wir	ihr	sie/ Sie
sein						
werden						
bleiben						
kommen						
geben						
fahren						
laufen						
ankommen						
abfahren						
fliegen						
wachsen						
sterben						
steigen						
einsteigen						
aussteigen						
umsteigen						
geschehen						
einziehen						
ausziehen						
umziehen						
fallen						
reiten						
springen						
stürzen						
passieren						
schwimmen						
zusammenstoßen						
aufstehen						
folgen						
reisen						
wandern						

In den folgenden Listen findest du die 70 wichtigsten deutschen Verben, die Perfekt, Plusquamperfekt und Futur II mit sein bilden.

Bewegungsverben

Folgende Verben der BeWegung werden als intransitive Verben (ohne Akkusativobjekt) mit sein gebildet. Das betrifft auch davon abgeleitete Verben, die eine BeWegung ausdrücken:

Beispiel:
fahren → Wir sind nach Berlin gefahren.
abfahren → Der Zug ist abgefahren.

Verb	Partizip II PERFEKT	Beispiel
abbiegen	abgebogen	Ich bin an der Kreuzung falsch abgebogen.
ausweichen	ausgewichen	Er ist dem Hindernis ausgewichen.
fahren	gefahren	Wir sind an den See gefahren.
fallen	gefallen	Die Tasse ist vom Tisch gefallen.
fliegen	geflogen	Die Vögel sind schon in den Süden geflogen.
fliehen	geflohen	Viele Revolutionäre sind ins Ausland geflohen.
fliessen	geflossen	Die Abwässer sind ungefiltert ins Meer geflossen.
flüchten	geflüchtet	Die Tiere sind vor dem Feuer geflüchtet.
folgen	gefolgt	Ich weiß, wo er arbeitet. Ich bin ihm heimlich gefolgt.
gehen	ge.gangen	Meine Eltern sind ins Theater ge.gangen.
hüpfen	gehüpft	Die Keinder sind auf einem Bein gehüpft.
joggen*	gejoggt	Wir sind heute Morgen durch den Park gejoggt.
klettern*	geklettert	Vera ist auf den Baum geklettert.
kommen	gekommen	Wann seid ihr gestern nach Hause gekommen?
kriechen	gekrochen	Mir ist eine Schnecke über die Hand gekrochen.
landen	gelandet	Ist das Flugzeug schon gelandet?
laufen	gelaufen	Wie oft bist du um den See gelaufen?
paddeln	gepaddelt	Wir sind in einem Schlauchboot auf der Elbe gepaddelt.
reisen	gereist	Sie ist in ihrem Leben viel gereist.
reiten	geritten	Die Reiter sind durch den Wald geritten.
rennen	gerannt	Ich bin gerannt, um den Bus nicht zu verpassen.
rudern	gerudert	Er ist über den See gerudert.
schwimmen*	geschwommen	Früher ist sie viel geschwommen.
se.geln	gese.gelt	Das Schiff ist nach Hamburg gese.gelt.
sinken	gesunken	Die Titanic ist 1912 gesunken.
springen	gesprungen	Das Keind ist in jede Pfütze gesprungen.
steigen	gestiegen	Am Morgen sind wir auf den Berg gestiegen.
starten	gestartet	Das Flugzeug ist gestartet.
stolpern	gestolpert	Ich bin über den Teppich gestolpert.
stürzen	gestürzt	Der Motorradfahrer ist gestürzt.
tauchen*	getaucht	Sie sind bis auf den Meeresgrund getaucht.
treten	getreten	Er ist in einen Nagel getreten.
wandern	gewandert	Wir sind gestern 25 Kilometer gewandert.
zurückkehren	zurückgekehrt	Unsere Nachbarn sind noch nicht aus dem Urlaub zurückgekehrt.
ziehen	gezogen	Mein Freund ist nach München gezogen.

* Diese Verben können das Perfekt auch mit haben bilden, wenn die Ortsänderung nicht im Vordergrund steht, siehe BeWegungsverben mit haben oder sein.

Übergang von einem Zustand in einen anderen

Folgende Verben kennzeichnen einen Übergang von einem Zustand in einen anderen.

Beispiel:
liegen/sitzen → aufstehen → stehen
Ich bin heute sehr früh aufgestanden.

Verb	Partizip II	Beispiel
aufstehen	aufgestanden	Wann *seid* ihr heute *aufgestanden*?
aufwachen	aufgewacht	Vom lauten Knall *ist* das Keind *aufgewacht*.
einschlafen	eingeschlafen	ich *bin* gestern vor dem Fernseher *eingeschlafen*.
explodieren	explodiert	Zum Glück *ist* die Bombe nicht *explodiert*.
gefrieren	gefroren	Es ist so kalt – der Tee in meiner Tasse *ist gefroren*.
platzen	geplatzt	Der Luftballon *ist geplatzt*.
schlüpfen	geschlüpft	Aus den Eiern *sind* Küken *geschlüpft*.
schwellen	geschwollen	Meine Hand ist geschwollen.
stehenbleiben	stehengeblieben	Das Auto *ist* mitten auf der Straße *stehengeblieben*.
sterben	gestorben	Der Schauspieler *ist* vor zwei Jahren *gestorben*.
tauen	getaut	Das Eis auf dem See *ist getaut*.
umfallen	umgefallen	Die Vase ist umgefallen.
verblühen	verblüht	Die Rose ist verblüht.
verschwinden	verschwunden	Die Sonne ist hinter den Wolken verschwunden.
wachsen	gewachsen	Ich muss zum Friseur. Meine Haare *sind* so schnell *gewachsen*.
zerfallen	zerfallen	Nachdem das Schloss verlassen wurde, *ist* es *zerfallen*.

Weitere Verben

Verb	Partizip II	Beispiel
auffallen	aufgefallen	Mir ist der Fehler sofort aufgefallen.
ausfallen	ausgefallen	Heute ist der Unterricht ausgefallen.
begegnen	begegnet	Sie kommen mir bekannt vor. Sind wir uns schon begegnet?
bleiben	geblieben	Seid ihr gestern zu Hause geblieben?
durchfallen	durchgefallen	Hast du die Prüfung bestanden oder bist du durchgefallen?
eintreffen	eingetroffen	Die Katastrophe ist zum Glück nicht eingetroffen.
entstehen	entstanden	Wie sind eigentlich die Alpen entstanden?
ersticken	erstickt	Mach endlich das Fenster auf, sonst bist du in zehn Minuten erstickt!
ertrinken	ertrunken	Beim Baden im See ist jemand ertrunken.
gelingen	gelungen	Es ist mir nicht gelungen, ihn zu überzeugen.
geschehen	geschehen	Was geschehen ist, ist geschehen.
Mißlingen	mißlungen	Sei nicht traurig. Jedem ist einmal etwas mißlungen.
passieren	passiert	Was ist in der Zwischenzeit passiert?
sein	gewesen	Seid ihr gestern im Keino gewesen?
verhungern	verhungert	Es ist niemand verhungert.
verzweifeln	verzweifelt	Auf der Suche nach dem Dokument bin ich fast verzweifelt.
vorkommen	vorgekommen	Es ist mehrfach vorgekommen, dass das Internet ausfällt.
Wegfallen	Weggefallen	Nach der Maueröffnung sind die Grenzkontrollen Weggefallen.
werden	geworden	Sie ist eine berühmte Wissenschaftlerin geworden.

Hier lernt ihr die 70 wichtigsten Verben, die das Perfekt sowohl mit haben als auch mit sein bilden können, mit Beispielen und Übungen.

Bevor ihr euch anseht, welche Verben das Perfekt sowohl mit haben als auch mit sein bilden können, empfehlen wir euch, noch einmal zu lesen, welche Verben das Perfekt mit haben und welche mit sein bilden.

Perfekt mit haben oder sein? – Erklärungen, Listen und Übungen

Verben, die eine Fortbewegung ausdrücken

Verben, die eine Fortbewegung, eine Bewegung in eine Richtung oder auf ein Ziel hin ausdrücken, bilden das Perfekt mit sein.

Stehen diese Verben aber mit einem Akkusativ, so bilden sie das Perfekt mit haben.

Wenn diese Verben **keine** Fortbewegung, sondern eher die Aktivität ausdrücken und nicht mit einem Akkusativ stehen (können), so können wir das Perfekt meistens mit sein und haben bilden.

70 wichtigsten Verben

fahren
Wir sind mit dem Auto zur Arbeit gefahren. (intransitiv; FortbeWegung)
Ich habe das Auto in die Garage gefahren. (transitiv)

fliegen
Wir sind nach Wien geflogen. Wir sind schon oft geflogen. (intransitiv; FortbeWegung)
Wer hat das Flugzeug geflogen, der Pilot oder der Co-Pilot? (transitiv)

reiten
Früher ist er jeden Tag geritten. (intransitiv; Fortbewegung)
Er war ein bisschen nervös, denn dieses neu Pferd hatte er noch nie geritten. (transitiv)

rudern
Wir sind über den See gerudert. (intransitiv; FortbeWegung)
Er hat die Vorräte auf die Insel gerudert. (transitiv)
Beim Laufen hat er mit den Armen gerudert. (Bedeutung: die Arme kreisförmig beWegen)

schwimmen
Wir sind durch den Fluss geschwommen. (Fortbewegung)
Wir sind/haben eine halbe Stunde geschwommen. (ohne Ziel, Aktivität)

segeln
Wir sind zum Hafen gese.gelt. (Fortbewegung)
Wir sind/haben stundenlang gesegelt. (ohne Ziel; Aktivität)

springen
Sie ist über das Hindernis gesprungen. (Bewegung)
Er ist/hat dreimal gesprungen. (Bedeutung: einen Sprung ausführen)
Er hat/ist einen neün Rekord gesprungen.

surfen
Der Surfer ist zurück zum Strand gesurft. (Fortbewegung)
Gestern haben/sind wir den ganzen Tag gesurft. (ohne Ziel; Aktivität)
Ich habe die ganze Nacht im Internet gesurft. (Aktivität)

tanzen
Wir sind durch das Zimmer getanzt. (Fortbewegung)
Wir haben viel getanzt. Wir haben Tango getanzt. (transitiv)

tauchen
Wir sind bis zum Meeresboden getaucht. (Fortbewegung)
Sie ist 23 Meter tief getaucht. (Fortbewegung)

Wir haben/sind gestern wieder getaucht. (Aktivität)
Er hat/ist über zwei Minuten getaucht. (Aktivität; Dauer)

Andere Verben, die das Perfekt mit haben und sein bilden.Sind die folgenden Verben intransitiv, d.h. sie haben **kein** Akkusativobjekt, wird das Perfekt mit sein gebildet.

Wenn die folgenden Verben transitiv sind, also mit einem Akkusativ stehen (können), bilden wir das Perfekt mit - - haben.

Auch wenn die Verben reflexiv sind, bilden wir das Perfekt mit - haben.
In manchen Fällen werden mit haben oder sein aber auch nur Bedeutungsunterschiede geschaffen.

abbrechen
Der Ast ist abgebrochen. (intransitiv)
Der Sänger hat das Konzert wegen des Regens abgebrochen. (transitiv)
ebenso: durchbrechen, zerbrechen

abhauen
Die Einbrecher sind mit der Beute abgehauen. (intransitiv; Bewegung)
Er hat den Eiszapfen mit einem Stock abgehauen. (transitiv)

abknicken
Der Ast ist abgeknickt. (intransitiv)
Er hat ein Stück abgeknickt. (transitiv)

abtreten
Der große Schauspieler *ist* von der Bühne des Lebens abgetreten. (intransitiv)

Er hat das Grundstück an seine Nachbarn abgetreten. (transitiv)
anfahren
Plötzlich ist der Wagen angefahren. (intransitiv)
Der Fahrer hat einen Fußgänger angefahren. (transitiv)

anfallen
Bei dem Fest ist sehr viel Müll angefallen. (intransitiv)
Der Hund hat den Spaziergänger angefallen. (transitiv)

anstoßen
Es war sehr niedrig und er ist mit dem Kopf angestoßen. (Bedeutung: gegen etwas stoßen)
Wir haben mit Sekt auf seinen Geburtstag angestoßen. (Bedeutung: sich zuprosten)

auftreten
Der erfolgreiche Sänger ist im In- und Ausland aufgetreten. (intransitiv)
Informieren Sie mich bitte, sollten Probleme auftreten. (intransitiv)
Die Tür war verschlossen, aber er hat sie aufgetreten. (transitiv)

aufziehen
Den ganzen Tag lang war das Wetter wunderbar, doch am Abend sind Gewitterwolken aufgezogen. (intransitiv; Bewegung)
Sie haben drei Keinder aufgezogen. (transitiv)

ausfahren
Am Wochenende sind wir mit der Familie ausgefahren. (intransitiv)
Der junge Mann hat jeden Morgen die Zeitung ausgefahren. (transitiv)

ausklingen
Der Abend ist sehr schön und harmonisch ausgeklungen. (Bedeutung: langsam enden)
Die Glocken haben ausgeklungen. (Bedeutung: aufhören zu klingen)

ausreißen
Der Jugendliche ist von zu Hause ausgerissen. (intransitiv; BeWegung)
Der Gärtner hat das Unkraut ausgerissen. (transitiv)

ausscheiden

Durch die Niederlage ist die Mannschaft aus dem Turnier ausgeschieden. (intransitiv)
Der Körper hat die aufgenommenen Schadstoffe wieder ausgeschieden. (transitiv)

ausziehen
Wir sind aus der Wohnung ausgezogen. (intransitiv)
Ich habe mir die Jacke ausgezogen. (transitiv)

bekommen
Mir ist übel. Ich glaube, das Essen ist mir nicht bekommen. (intransitiv)
Ich habe eine Einladung zur Hochzeit bekommen. (transitiv)

biegen
Er ist mit dem Auto um die Kurve geboren. (intransitiv; Bewegung)
Er hat den Stab so weit gebogen, bis er ganz krumm war. (transitiv)

bleichen
Der Stoff ist im Sonnenlicht geblichen. (intransitiv; Bedeutung: bleich werden)
Die Frau hat ihre Haare gebleicht. (transitiv; Bedeutung: bleich machen)

brechen
Das Eis ist gebrochen. Er ist durch das Eis gebrochen. (intransitiv)
Er hat sein Wort gebrochen. (transitiv)
Er hat gebrochen. (Bedeutung: sich übergeben)

dringen
Sie sind durch das dichte Gestrüpp gedrungen. (intransitiv; Bewegung)
Sie wollten ihr Geld sofort bekommen und haben deshalb auf eine schnelle Zahlung gedrungen. (Bedeutung:
fordern)

durchbrennen
Der Junge ist mit seiner Freundin durchgebrannt. (Bedeutung: weglaufen)
Die Sicherung ist durchgebrannt. (Bedeutung: schmelzen)
Die Lampe hat die ganze Nacht durchgebrannt. (Bedeutung: ohne Unterbrechung
brennen)

durchfliegen
Ich bin bei der Prüfung durchgeflogen. (intransitiv; Bedeutung: durchfallen; nicht bestehen)
Das Flugzeug hat die Wolkendecke durchflogen. (transitiv: Bedeutung: durch etwas fliegen)

einfrieren
Der Fisch ist im Eis eingefroren. (intransitiv)
Es war so kalt, daß die Wasserleitungen eingefroren sind. (intransitiv)
Wir haben die Reste vom Mittagessen in der Tiefkühltruhe eingefroren. (transitiv)

eintreten
Die Tür hat sich geöffnet und er ist eingetreten. (intransitiv)
Das, was er befürchtet hatte, ist nun eingetreten. (intransitiv)
Er hat die Tür mit dem Fuß eingetreten. (transitiv)

einziehen
Letzten Monat sind sie in die neu Wohnung eingezogen. (intransitiv)
Sie haben Erkundigungen über alle Bewerber eingezogen. (transitiv)

erschrecken
Er ist erschrocken. (intransitiv)
Der Junge hat seine kleine Schwester erschreckt. (transitiv)
Ich habe mich sehr erschreckt. (reflexiv)

folgen
Er ist ihm bis nach Hause gefolgt. (intransitiv; FortbeWegung)
Ein Unglück ist auf das andere gefolgt. (intransitiv)
Die Keinder haben den Eltern mal wieder nicht gefolgt. (Bedeutung: gehorchen)

frieren
Das Wasser ist gefroren. (Bedeutung: zu Eis werden)
Ich habe gefroren. (Bedeutung: Kälte empfinden)

heilen
Die Wunde ist geheilt. (intransitiv)
Der Arzt hat die Wunde geheilt. (transitiv)

jagen
Der Skifahrer ist in einem Wahnsinnstempo über die Piste gejagt. (intransitiv; BeWegung)
Früher hat mein Onkel Hasen gejagt. (transitiv)

rollen
Die Kugel ist in das Loch gerollt. (intransitiv)
Ich habe den Ball über den Boden gerollt. (transitiv)

scheiden
Man vermutet, dass er nicht freiwillig aus dem Leben geschieden ist. (intransitiv)
Man hat das Paar nach nur drei Monaten wieder geschieden. (transitiv)

scheren
Er ist mit seinem Motorrad nach links geschert. (intransitiv; Bewegung)
Der Schäfer hat seine Schafe geschoren. (transitiv)
Es hat ihn nie geschert, was die Leute denken. (transitiv; Bedeutung: intereßieren; kümmern)

schießen
Das Auto ist plötzlich um die Ecke geschossen. (intransitiv)
Heute hat der Fußballer sein erstes Tor geschossen. (transitiv)

schmelzen
Der Schnee ist geschmolzen. (intransitiv)
Die Sonne hat das Eis geschmolzen. (transitiv)

schwingen
Der Artist ist am Trapez durch das Zirkuszelt geschwungen. (intransitiv; BeWegung)
Die begeisterten Fans haben ihre Fahnen geschwungen. (transitiv)

starten
Das Flugzeug ist um 17.34 Uhr gestartet. (intransitiv)
Der Fahrer hat den Motor gestartet. (transitiv)

stossen
Er ist mit dem Kopf an die Decke gestossen. (Bewegung)
Er hat das Glass vom Tisch gestossen. (transitiv)

streichen
Er ist durch Wälder und Felder gestrichen. (intransitiv; Bedeutung: ohne bestimmtes Ziel wandern)
Wir haben unser Wohnzimmer gestrichen. (transitiv; Bedeutung: anstreichen; anmalen)

treiben
Das Floß ist über den Fluß getrieben. (intransitiv; Fortbewegung)
Früher habe ich viel Sport getrieben. (transitiv)
Der Hirte hat seine Schafe auf die Wiese getrieben. (transitiv)

treten
Er ist in die Pfütze getreten. Er ist über die Linie getreten. (intransitiv, BeWegung)
Er hat ihn getreten. (transitiv)

treten (auf/gegen…)
Er ist/hat mir auf den Fuß getreten. (ohne Absicht)
Er hat mir auf den Fuß getreten. (mit Absicht)
Er ist/hat gegen den Stein getreten. (ein Tritt ohne Absicht)
Er hat gegen den Ball getreten. (ein Tritt mit Absicht)

trocknen
Die Wäsche ist in der Sonne getrocknet. (intransitiv)
Ich habe meine Haare mit dem Föhn getrocknet. (transitiv)

überlaufen
Das Waschbecken ist übergelaufen. Er ist zum Feind übergelaufen. (intransitiv)
Er war schneller und hat den Gegner überlaufen. (transitiv)

übersteigen
Die Diebe sind vom Balkon der Nachbarwohnung auf unseren übergestiegen. (intransitiv; Bewegung;
hinübersteigen)
Diese unglaublich hohen Zahlen haben meine Vorstellungskraft überstiegen. (transitiv)

übertreten
Der Fluß ist übergetreten. (intransitiv)
Der Weitspringer ist übergetreten. (intransitiv)
Er hat das Gesetz übertreten. (transitiv)

umgehen
Er ist mit dem Gerät nicht vorsichtig umge.gangen. (intransitiv; Bedeutung: behandeln)
Ich habe es umgangen, ihm zu begegnen. Wir haben das Hindernis umgangen. (transitiv; Bedeutung:
vermeiden; einen Bogen um etwas machen)

umziehen
Sie sind schon wieder umgezogen. Sie wohnen nie länger als ein paar Jahre an einem Ort. (intransitiv;
Bewegung)
Nach der Arbeit habe ich mich zu Hause umgezogen. (reflexiv)

unterlaufen
Mir ist ein Fehler unterlaufen. (intransitiv)
Der Torwart hat die Flanke unterlaufen. (transitiv)

verbrennen
Das Holz ist vollständig verbrannt. (intransitiv)
Er hat den Müll verbrannt. (transitiv)

verderben
Das Essen ist verdorben. (intransitiv)
Er hat uns den Spaß verdorben. (transitiv)

verfahren
Sie sind sehr ungerecht mit ihm verfahren. (intransitiv; Bedeutung: umgehen, handeln)
Wir hatten **keinen** Stadtplan dabei und haben uns verfahren. (reflexiv; Bedeutung: den falschen Weg nehmen)

vorfahren
Wir sind bis an die Spitze vorgefahren. (intransitiv)
Der Chauffeur hat das Auto vorgefahren. (transitiv)

vorschießen
Sie ist ganz unerwartet hinter der Mauer vorgeschossen. (intransitiv; Bewegung)
Ich brauchte Geld. Zum Glück hat mir mein Arbeitgeber einen Teil meines nächsten Monatslohns
vorgeschossen. (transitiv)

wechseln
Der Spieler ist zu einem anderen Verein gewechselt. (intransitiv)
Der Spieler hat den Verein gewechselt. (transitiv)

Wegziehen
Er wohnt nicht mehr hier. Er ist vor ein paar Monaten weggezogen. (intransitiv; BeWegung)
Als er mit dem anderen Mann in Streit geriet, haben seine Freunde ihn

Weggezogen,
um eine Schlägerei zu verhindern. (transitiv)

ziehen
Wir sind nach Berlin gezogen. Sie sind durch die Altstadt gezogen. (intransitiv)
Die Lokomotive hat die Waggons gezogen. (transitiv)

zurücktreten
Der Politiker ist von seinem Amt zurückgetreten. (Bedeutung: sein Amt abgeben)
Er wurde getreten und hat zurückgetreten. (Bedeutung: einen Tritt mit einem Tritt beantworten)

zusammentreten
Das Parlament ist zusammengetreten. (intransitiv)
Der brutale Schläger hat sein Opfer zusammengetreten. (transitiv).

zustoßen
Was ist passiert? Hoffentlich ist ihm nichts zugestoßen. (Bedeutung: passieren)
Er hat mit dem Messer zugestoßen und seine Gegenüber schwer verletzt. (Bedeutung: mit einem Stich verletzen)

zuziehen
Sie wohnen seit einem Monat hier im Dorf. Sie sind neu zugezogen. (intransitiv; Bewegung)
Am Abend hat sie die Vorhänge zugezogen. (transitiv)

Verbs- Dativ, Akkusativ, Dativ/ Akkusativ
Rule: With Person: Dativ, E.g. Ich schreibe meinem Vater

With Things: Akkusativ E.g. Ich schreibe einen Brief
Dativ/ Akkusativ: Ich schreibe meinem Vater einen Brief.

Dativ		
Gehen (es geht)		
antworten		
danken		
gefallen		
gehören		
fehlen		
folgen		
einfallen		
gelingen		
gratulieren		
helfen		
passen		
schaden		
schmecken		
raten		
ähneln		
Bege.gnen		
dienen		
vertrauen		
sagen		
Akkusativ		
haben		
benutzen		
bezahlen		
einladen		
fragen		

finden		
geben		
hören		
kennen		
lernen		
lesen		
lieben		
machen		
nehmen		
spielen		
stören		
suchen		
besuchen		
treffen		
essen		
trinken		
brauchen		
sehen		
verkaufen		
anrufen		
einkaufen		
gewinnen		
grüßen		
hassen		
Dativ / Akkusativ		
bringen		
erklären		
erzielen		
geben		
lassen		
leiten		
melden		
schenken		
schreiben		
senden		
vorlesen		
vorstellen		
wünschen		
zahlen		
kaufen		
wünschen		
zahlen		
kaufen		
Waschen		

Präsens		Präteritum	Perfekt	Plusquamperfekt	Futur I	Futur II
ich	frage	fragte	habe gefragt	hatte gefragt	werde fragen	werde gefragt haben

du	fragst	fragtest	hast gefragt	hattest gefragt	wirst fragen	wirst gefragt haben
er/sie/es	fragt	fragte	hat gefragt	hatte gefragt	wird fragen	wird gefragt haben
wir	fragen	fragten	haben gefragt	hatten gefragt	werden fragen	werden gefragt haben
ihr	fragt	fragtet	habt gefragt	hattet gefragt	werdet fragen	werdet gefragt haben
sie/Sie	fragen	fragten	haben gefragt	hatten gefragt	werden fragen	werden gefragt haben

Subjunctive   **Indikativ Konjunktiv I**

Präsens		Perfekt	Futur I	Futur II
ich	frage	habe gefragt	werde fragen	werde gefragt haben
du	fragest	habest gefragt	werdest fragen	werdest gefragt haben
er/sie/es	frage	habe gefragt	werde fragen	werde gefragt haben
wir	fragen	haben gefragt	werden fragen	werden gefragt haben
ihr	fraget	habet gefragt	werdet fragen	werdet gefragt haben
sie/Sie	fragen	haben gefragt	werden fragen	werden gefragt haben

Konjunktiv II (Imperativ)

Ge.genwart		würde-Form	Vergangenheit	Ge.genwart	
ich	fragte	würde fragen	hätte gefragt	(du)	Frag(e)!
du	fragtest	würdest fragen	hättest gefragt	(Sie)	Fragen Sie!
er/sie/es	fragte	würde fragen	hätte gefragt	(wir)	Fragen wir!
wir	fragten	würden fragen	hätten gefragt	(ihr)	Fragt!
ihr	fragtet	würdet fragen	hättet gefragt		
sie/Sie	fragten		hätten gefragt		

Infinite Formen
        Infinitiv   sein
        Partizip   gewesen

Indikativ

Präsens		Präteritum	Perfekt	Plusquamperfekt	Futur I	Futur II
ich	komme an	kam an	bin angekommen	war angekommen	werde ankommen	werde angekommen sein
du	kommst an	kamst an	bist angekommen	Warst angekommen	wirst ankommen	wirst angekommen sein
er/sie/es	kommt an	kam an	ist angekommen	war angekommen	wird ankommen	wird angekommen sein
wir	kommen an	kamen an	sind angekommen	waren angekommen	werden ankommen	werden angekommen sein
ihr	kommt an	kamt an	seid angekommen	wart angekommen	werdet ankommen	werdet angekommen sein
sie/Sie	kommen an	kamen an	sind angekommen	waren angekommen	werden ankommen	werden angekommen sein

	Konjunktiv I				Konjunktiv II			Imperativ	
	Präsens	Perfekt	Futur I	Futur II	Ge.genwart	würde-Form	Vergangenheit	Ge.genwart	
ich	komme an	sei angekommen	werde ankommen	werde angekommen sein	käme an	würde ankommen	wäre angekommen	(du)	Komm(e) an
du	kommest an	seist angekommen	werdest ankommen	werdest angekommen sein	käm(e)st an	würdest ankommen	wär(e)st angekommen	(Sie)	Kommen Sie an
er/sie/es	komme an	sei angekommen	werde ankommen	werde angekommen sein	käme an	würde ankommen	wäre angekommen	(wir)	Kommen wir an
wir	kommen an	seien angekommen	werden ankommen	werden angekommen sein	kämen an	würden ankommen	wären angekommen	(ihr)	Kommt an
ihr	kommet an	seiet angekommen	werdet ankommen	werdet angekommen sein	käm(e)t an	würdet ankommen	wär(e)t angekommen		
sie/Sie	kommen an	seien angekommen	werden ankommen	werden angekommen sein	kämen an	würden ankommen	wären angekommen		

(Overprinted over the table above:)

Infinite Formen	
Infinitiv	haben
Partizip	gehabt

Indikativ

Präsens	Präteritum	Perfekt	Plusquamperfekt	Futur I	Futur II	Präsens
ich	habe	hatte	habe gehabt	hatte gehabt	werde haben	werde gehabt haben
du	hast	hattest	hast gehabt	hattest gehabt	wirst haben	wirst gehabt haben
er/sie/es	hat	hatte	hat gehabt	hatte gehabt	wird haben	wird gehabt haben
wir	haben	hatten	haben gehabt	hatten gehabt	werden haben	werden gehabt haben
ihr	habt	hattet	habt gehabt	hattet gehabt	werdet haben	werdet gehabt haben
sie/Sie	haben	hatten	haben gehabt	hatten gehabt	werden haben	werden gehabt haben

Infinite Formen	
Infinitiv	antworten
Partizip	geantwortet

Präsens		Präteritum		Perfekt	
ich	antworte	ich	antwortete	ich	habe geantwortet
du	antwortest	du	antwortetest	du	hast geantwortet
er/sie/es	antwortet	er/sie/es	antwortete	er/sie/es	hat geantwortet
wir	antworten	wir	antworteten	wir	haben geantwortet
ihr	antwortet	ihr	antwortetet	ihr	habt geantwortet
sie/Sie	antworten	sie/Sie	antworteten	sie/Sie	haben geantwortet

	Präsens	Perfekt	Futur I	Futur II	Ge.genwart	würde-Form	Vergangenheit		Ge.genwart
ich	habe	habe gehabt	werde haben	werde gehabt haben	hätte	würde haben	hätte gehabt	(du)	Hab(e)!
du	hast	habest gehabt	werdest haben	werdest gehabt haben	hättest	würdest haben	hättest gehabt	(Sie)	Haben Sie!
er/sie/es	hat	habe gehabt	werde haben	werde gehabt haben	hätte	würde haben	hätte gehabt	(wir)	Haben wir!
wir	haben	haben gehabt	werden haben	werden gehabt haben	hätten	würden haben	hätten gehabt	(ihr)	Habt!
ihr	habt	habet gehabt	werdet haben	werdet gehabt haben	hättet	würdet haben	hättet gehabt		
sie/Sie	haben	haben gehabt	werden haben	werden gehabt haben	hätten	würden haben	hätten gehabt		

Infinite Formen	
Infinitiv	besuchen
Partizip	besucht

Präsens		Präteritum		Perfekt	
ich	besuche	ich	besuchte	ich	habe besucht
du	besuchst	du	besuchtest	du	hast besucht
er/sie/es	besucht	er/sie/es	besuchte	er/sie/es	hat besucht

Präsens		Präteritum		Perfekt	
wir	besuchen	wir	besuchten	wir	haben besucht
ihr	besucht	ihr	besuchtet	ihr	habt besucht
sie/Sie	besuchen	sie/Sie	besuchten	sie/Sie	haben besucht

Infinite Formen	
Infinitiv	ankommen
Partizip	angekommen

Präsens		Präteritum		Perfekt	
ich	komme an	ich	kam an	ich	bin angekommen
du	kommst an	du	kamst an	du	bist angekommen
er/sie/es	kommt an	er/sie/es	kam an	er/sie/es	ist angekommen
wir	kommen an	wir	kamen an	wir	sind angekommen
ihr	kommt an	ihr	kamt an	ihr	seid angekommen
sie/Sie	kommen an	sie/Sie	kamen an	sie/Sie	sind angekommen

Prepositions

As the name suggests- before position i.e. a word which before position ie. a word which comes before position to show the position of the word.

In other words it shows the connection between the two things that where, how and when these are connected with each other. E.g. The pen is on the table.

There is a connection between the pen and the table. That is: The pen is on the table.

In German there are 4 kinds of Prepositions:

1	Dativ
2	Akkusativ
3	Akkusativ and Dativ
4	Genetiv

To learn and understand it quickly, as abbreviations of each category has been used

1 Dativ: Von Zu S N A M B A G

V	Von	from, off, of, by, of (possessive)
Z	Zu	to, at, for
S	Seit	since
N	Nach	to, after, according to, past (time)
A	Aus	from, off, of, for, out of, made of)
M	Mit	with, by
B	Bei	at, with, near (to, at, for (in/ by with work), by
A	Onwards	
G	Gegenüber	Opposite to, access from

As some prepositions have the same meaning, it would be better to divide these into four parts

Aus	Von
Nach	zu
Mit	bei
seit	gegenüber

2 Akkusativ F U D B O G E

F	Für	for, by
U	Um	around, at
D	Durch	through, by
B	Bis	till, upto, to, by (with time)
O	Ohne	without
G	Gegen	against, around, into
E	Entlang	along (with)

3 Akkusativ and Dativ A A H U U V I N Z

A	an	on, at, at the edge of
A	auf	on, in (language)
H	hinter	behind
U	Unter	under, among
U	Über	under, among

V	Vor	in front of, before, to (time)
T		in, into, to, inside
N	Neben	next to, besides
Z	Zwishen	between

Use of Wechsel - what to use- Akk or Dattiv
If there is motion in the sentence, it will take Akkusativ.
If there is no motion in the sentence, it will take Dativ

E.g. - Ich le.ge dsa Buch auf den Tisch. (legen - motion - hence, Akkustive
Das Buch liegt auf dem Ticsh. (liegen - no motion -static - Hence, Dative)

4 Dativ   S T W W

Statt	instead of
Trotz	inspite of
Wegen	Because of
Waehrend	During

There are a few verbs which use fixed possessive with itself.
These are called "verbs with fixed preposition.

However, all the prepositions are from these cate.gories only so there is no new possessive to learn

e.g., Warten Auf + Akk
     Beginnen Mit + Dat.
     All rules already mentioned at " Verbs with fixed prepositions.

Präposition - Dativ

1 Aus - from, of, for,out of, made of
          a   from (place of origin)
          E.g., Ich komme aus Indien.
          b   Out of (from a closed place/ space/ room)
          E.g. Das Keind aus dem Haus.
          Er triknkt Waser aus dem Glass.
          c   made of (article not used)
          E.g., Der Tisch aus Holz.
          d   out of, for
          E.g., Aus diesem Grund kommt er heute nicht.
          Das Keind tut es aus Gewohnheit.

2   Von- from, off, of, by , of (possessive)
          a   from (not the origin)
          E.G., Er kommt von Neu Delhi.
          Ich habe ein Geschenk von meiner Frau bekommen.
          Bettina fällt von Stuhl.
          b   By
          Diese Buch wird von mir gelesen.
          c   of (posessive)
          E.g,. Er is ein Freund von mir.

3   NACH - To, after, according to, past (time)
          a   to (with big places, outside city)
          E.g., Sie fliegt nach Deutschland,
          b   After
          E.g., Er kommt nach dem Unterricht.

          c   Past (after)
          E.g., Es ist zehn nach Neun.
          d   According
          E.g., Nach ihm ist heute Sonntag.

4   ZU - to, at, for

    a.   To (with smallplaces inside the city and persons)
              E.g., Wir gchcn zum Markt.
              Er geht zu seinen Eltern.

    b.   at, for (occasion etc)
              E.g., Er kommt zu Diwali.
              Die Keinder gehen zum ersten mal in die Schule.

    c.   at (price of, for)

        E.g., Sie kauft das Bild zu hundert Dollar.

5.   MIT - With, by

    a   WITH
              e.g., Die Frau geht mit ihrem Mann.
              Sie wohnt mit seinem Onkel.
    b   BY - Transport
              e.g., Sie kommt mit dem Zug.

6.   Bei - at, with, near (to) for (in/by with work), by

    a.   AT, WITH
              e.g., Das Keind wohnt ei seinen Eltern.
    b.   NEAR
              e.g., Das Keino liegt bei unserer Schule.
    c.   AT (with Profession or business.
              e.g., Sie ist beim Zahnarzt. She is at dentist.

    d. - AT, FOR (in/by - workeing in a company /Organisation etc.
              e.g., Ich arbeite beim IBM
    e. - BY, In process of
              e.g., Beim schreiben macht man Fehler.

7.   Seit - since
              e.g., Seit einem Monat wohnt sie hier.

8.   GEGENÜBER - opposite to, access from
    e.g., Meine Frau sitzt mir gegenüber.

9.   Some special and idiomatic uses

    Er is zu Haus.   He is at home
    Er geht nach Haus.   He is going home
    Er kommt vom zu   Haus. He is coming from home.
    Er geht zu Fuß.   He is going on foot.

Possessive Akkusativ

    1.   FÜR- for, by
         a.   For
         b.   BY

    2.   UM - around, at
         a.   AROUND
         b.   AT

    3.   DURCH - through, by
         a.   THROUGH
         b.   By

    4   BIS - till, upto, to, by(with time)
         a.   TILL
         b.   TILL / Upto/ as far as
         c.   To
         d.   By

    5.   OHNE- Without

6 GEGEN- against, around, into
      a.   AGAINST
      b.   AROUND
      c.   INTO

7   ENTLANG - along (with) Postposition

Präposition Wechsel

a.   ON (vertical surface)
e.g. Ich hänge das Bild an die Wand.

I hang the picture on the wall.		Akk
od. Das Bild hängt an der Wand.	Dat	

b.   At, at the edge
E.g. Er steht an der Brücke.
He is standing on the bridge   Dat

Er stellt das Fahrrad an die Wand   Akk
Sie studiert an der Uni.
She is studying in the university.   Dat

a   ON - horizontal surface.
e.g. Tina legt das Buch auf den Stuhl.

Tina keeps the books on the chair.   Akk
Die Bücher liegen auf dem Tisch.
The books are lying on the table.   Dat

b   IN - language
         e.g. Sagen Sie es auf Deutsch, bitte.
         Please say it in English.   Akk
         Er schläft im Zimmer.
         He is sleeping in the room   Dat

E.g. Die Katze lauft hinter das Sofa
The cat is goes bhind the sofa.   Akk
Die Katze sitzt hinter dem Sofa.
The cat is sitting behind the sofa.   Dat

a   UNDER
         e.g. Das Keind spielt unter den Tisch.
         The child is playing under the table   Akk
         Das Keind sitzt unter dem Tisch.
         The child is sitting under the table   Dat

b   AMONG
         E.g., Das Gespräch unter den Mädchen heißt Klatsch
         The conversation among the girls is called gossip.
a   OVER , ABOVE
         E.g., Ich häng das Bild Über mein Beitt.
         I hang the picture above my bed.   Akk
         Das Bild hängt über mein Bett
         The picture is hanging over my bed.   Dat

         Der alte Mann ist über neunzig Jahre alt.
         The man is over ninety years old.

b   ACROSS, ON THE OTHER SIDE
         E.g., Das Mädchen geht über die Straße
         The girl is going across the street.   Akk
         Das Mädchen wartet über die Brücke.
         The girl is waiting on the bridge.   Dat

c   ABOUT
         E.g., Wir sprechen über das Wetter.
         We are speakeing about the weather.   Akk

a   IN FRONT OF
         e.g., Stellen Sie den Tisch vor die Wand.
         Put the table before / in front of the wall.   Akk

b   Der Tisch steht vor der Wand.
         The table is in front of the wall.   Dat

c   Before, to (time)
         e.g., Es is zehn vor neun.

         It is 10 (min) before/to nine.   Akk
         e.g., Schreiben Sie in das Heft.
         Write in the notebook.   Akk
         Das Wasser ist in der Flasche.
         The water is in the bottle   Dat

b   GOING to or BEING in a CLOSED / surrounded PLACE
         e.g.,
         Akk   Dat
         in die Schule   in der Schule
         in das Theater   In dem Theater
         in das Büro   In dem Büro

USED with some countries whose article is "DIE"

e.g.,

In die Schweiz	in der Schweiz
in die Türki	in der Türki
in die Tasche	in der Tasche
in die USA	in den USA

as Keind sitzt neben seinem Vater
he child is sitting next/ beside his father
is putting the chair between the table and the bed.   Akk
er Stuhl liegt zwischen dem Tisch und dem Bett
he chair is lying between the table and the bed.   Dat

oposition Genitiv

STATT - instead of
e.g., Statt des Geldes schickte sein Vater ihm die Bucher
TROTZ - in spite of
e.g., Trotz des warmen Tages trae.gt er einen Pulli.
WEGEN - because of, dü to
E.g., Wegen der Prüfung gehe ich nicht ins Keino.
WAEHREND
E.g., Waehernd der Nacht bleibe ich zu Haus

erbs with fixed Prepositions

owever, it must be noted that one should still read the full sentence to determine posessives as the verb may
ave been used in other sense.

e.g., arbeiten für +Akk - to work for something/ someone
Ich arbeite für meine Prüfung.

owever, if "arbeiten" has been used in the sense of workeing in a company etc., "BEI" must be used, as onl;y
BEI" can be used for this purpose.

ne does not need to learn the cases with these verbs with fixed prpositions as DATIV prepositions will take
ly DATIV case and AKKUSATIV only AKKUSATIV etc. and "WECHSEL PREPOSITIONS" mostly take
KKUSATIV case.
here are a few verbs which use two or more prepositions. In that case we should know the meaning / sense of
e sentence to determine the preposition.
g.,   Schreiben an - to write someone
Schreiben Über- to write about something.
Schreiben ab - to copy from somebody

Some verbs have two forms- SIMPLE and REFLEXIVE. Take care of the form which has been used in the sentence.

e.g.,   Sorgen für - to take care of, to look after
           sich sorgen um - to be worried about
           Er sorgt für seine Keinder.
           Er sorgt sich um ihre Keinder.

Verb	Preposition	English	Case
Abstimmen	über	to vote on	Accusative
Achten	auf	to pay attention to	Accusative
Antworten	auf	to reply to	Accusative
sich ärgern	über	to be annoyed about	Accusative
Aufpaßen	auf	to watch out for	Accusative
sich auf**Reg**en	über	to get upset / angry about	Accusative
Ausgeben	für	to spend (money) on	Accusative
sich bedanken	für	to thank for sth.	Accusative
Berichten	über	to report on	Accusative
sich beschweren	über	to complain about sth.	Accusative
sich bewerben	um	to apply for	Accusative
sich beziehen	auf	to refer to	Accusative
Bitten	um	to ask for	Accusative
Danken	für	to thank for	Accusative
Denken	an	to think of	Accusative
Diskutieren	über	to discuß sth.	Accusative
sich drehen	um	to revolve around	Accusative
sich entscheiden	für	to decide on	Accusative
sich entschuldigen	für	to apologize for	Accusative
Erinnern	an	to remind about	Accusative
sich erinnern	an	to remember	Accusative
Ersetzen	durch	to replace with	Accusative
sich freün	auf	to look forward to	Accusative
sich freün	über	to be pleased about	Accusative
Gehen	um	to be about	Accusative
sich gewöhnen	an	to get used to	Accusative
Glauben	an	to believe in	Accusative
Halten	für	to **Reg**ard sb. / sth. as	Accusative
sich handeln	um	to be about sth.	Accusative
Hören	auf	to listen to	Accusative
Hoffen	auf	to hope for	Accusative
(sich) informieren	über	to inform yourself about	Accusative
sich intereßieren	für	to be interested in	Accusative
Kämpfen	für	to fight for	Accusative
Kämpfen	gegen	to fight against	Accusative
sich konzentrieren	auf	to concentrate on	Accusative
sich kümmern	um	to look after sb. / sth.	Accusative
Lächeln	über	to smile about	Accusative
Lachen	über	to laugh about	Accusative
Nachdenken	über	to think about	Accusative
Protestieren	gegen	to protest against	Accusative
Reagieren	auf	to react to	Accusative
Reden	über	to talk about	Accusative

sich schämen	für	to be ashamed of	Accusative
Schimpfen	über	to complain about	Accusative
Schreiben	an	to write to	Accusative
Schreiben	über	to write about	Accusative
Sein	für	to agree with	Accusative
Sein	gegen	to disagree with	Accusative
Sorgen	für	to look after sb. / sth.	Accusative
Sprechen	über	to speak about	Accusative
Stehen	auf	to like sb. / sth.	Accusative
Stimmen	für	to vote for	Accusative
Stimmen	gegen	to vote against	Accusative
sich streiten	über	to argü about	Accusative
tun	für	to do for	Accusative
sich unterhalten	über	to chat about	Accusative
unterrichten	über	to teach about	Accusative
sich verlassen	auf	to depend on	Accusative
sich verlieben	in	to fall in love with	Accusative
vermieten	an	to rent to	Accusative
verzichten	auf	to go without sth.	Accusative
sich vorbereiten	auf	to prepare for	Accusative
warten	auf	to wait for	Accusative
sich wenden	an	to turn to sb.	Accusative
sich wundern	über	to wonder about	Accusative
abhängen	von	to depend on	Dative
anfangen	mit	to start with	Dative
arbeiten	an	to work on	Dative
arbeiten	bei	to work for (a company)	Dative
aufhören	mit	to stop with	Dative
sich bedanken	bei	to thank sb.	Dative
Beginnen	mit	to start with	Dative
sich beschäftigen	mit	to be busy with	Dative
sich beschweren	bei	to complain to sb.	Dative
bestehen	auf	to insist on	Dative
bestehen	aus	to consist of	Dative
einladen	zu	to invite to	Dative
sich entschuldigen	bei	to apologize to	Dative
sich erholen	von	to recover from	Dative
sich erkundigen	nach	to inquire about	Dative
erzählen	von	to tell sb. about	Dative
folgen	auf	to follow on	Dative
fragen	nach	to ask about	Dative
gehören	zu	to belong to	Dative
gratulieren	zu	to congratulate on	Dative
leiden	an	to suffer from	Dative
leiden	unter	to suffer dü to	Dative
reden	mit	to talk with	Dative
riechen	nach	to smell of	Dative
sprechen	mit	to speak with	Dative
sterben	an	to die of	Dative

sich streiten	mit	to argü with sb.	Dative
teilnehmen	an	to take part in	Dative
träumen	von	to dream of / about	Dative
sich treffen	mit	to meet up with	Dative
überzeugen	von	to convince sb. of	Dative
sich unterhalten	mit	to chat with	Dative
sich verabreden	mit	to arrange to meet with	Dative
sich verabschieden	von	to say goodbye to	Dative
zweifeln	an	to doubt sth.	Dative

Conjunction

Conjunction as the name implies joins words, sentence, phrase, and other units of language together.

There are 2 types of Conjunction

1 Subordinating conjunctions
2 Coordinating conjunctions

Coordinate conjunctions	Subordinate conjunctions			Compound conjunctions
aber	als	ob	sowie	weder .. noch
beziehungsweise	bevor	obwohl	während	anstatt..zu
denn	bis	seit	weil	entweder...oder
oder	dass	seitdem	wenn	sowohl ... als (auch)
sondern	damit	so bald	wie	sowohl ... wie (auch)
und	nachdem	so fern	wo	je ... desto
		soweit		zwar ... aber

Subordinating conjuntions

     These conjuntions affect the word order of the sentence in which this has been used, the verb which comes at the IInd place, goes to the end of sentence.
The word order becomes like changes to following:
Conjunction-
a. first sentence (verb at end) - , - verb of the second sentence - rest of the 2nd sentence

e.g., Wenn ich Geld habe (verb of the 1st sentence), gehe (verb of the 2nd sentence) ich ins Keino.

Das Wetter ist schlecht. Die Keinder gehen in die Schule.

Obwohl das Wetter schlecht ist, gehen die Keinder in die Schule.

Trots des schlechte Wetters, gehen die Keinder in die Schule.

b. If the conjunction comes in 2nd sentence, 1st Sentence - , - Conjunction - 2nd sentence (verb at end)

    e.g.,   Sie kann nicht tanzen. Sie ist krank.
    Sie kann nicht tanzen weil Sie krank ist.
    Er hat angerufen. Er kann nicht kommen.
    Er kann nicht kommen, weil er krank ist.

Coordinating conjunctions

These conjunctions do not affect the word order of the sentence.

e.g.,   Der President will hier kommen, Er hat **keine** Zeit.
    Der President will hier kommen, aber er hat **keine** Zeit.

To understand and learn the Conjunctions quickly, learn the abbreviations :

    W - WENN   IF
    W - WEIL BECAUSE
    W - WIE   AS, IF, HOW
    O - OB   WHETHER
    O - OBWOHL   ALTHOUGH
    D - Dass   THAT
    A – ALS   AS, IF

Subordinating conjunctions are little words that "subordinate" one clause to another. They cause the verb to go to the very end of the clause they are subordinating:

Conjunction	English	Example Sentence	English Translation
wenn	when (pres. & fut.), if	Wenn ich Geld habe fahre ich nach England.	If I have money, I will travel to England.
weil	because	Sie darf nicht tanzen, weil Sie krank ist.	She should not dance because she is sick.
wie	As, if, how		
ob	whether	Ich weiß es nicht, ob der Leher morgen einkaufen gehen kann.	I do not know if theach will go shopping tomorrow.
obwohl	although	Er kocht, obwohl er nicht kochen kann.	He is cookeing, although he can not cook.
daß	that	Ich glaube, dass seine Antwort falsch ist.	I think that his answer is wrong.
als	when (past)	Als ich jünger war, hatte ich einen Hund und zwei Katzen.	When I was younger, I had a dog and two cats.
als ob, als	as if	Er hat mich angeschaut, als ob er mich niemals im Leben gesehen hätte.	He looked at me as if he had never seen me before in his life.
wann	when (qüstion)	Ich weiß nicht, wann der Film anfängt. [implied qüstion - Wann fängt der Film an?]	I don't know when the film starts.
Statt.. zu		Er faehrt mit dem Bus, statt mit dem Auto zu fahren.	
ab			
bevor / ehe	before	Es gibt immer eine halbe Stunde Werbung, bevor der Film Beginnt.	There is always half an hour of advertisements before the film Begins.
bis	until, by (time)	Es daürt noch eine Stunde, bis ich fertig bin.	It'll be another hour until I'm finished.
da	as (because)	Er konnte das Geschenk nicht kaufen, da er nicht genug Geld hatte.	He couldn't buy the present, as he didn't have enough money.
damit	so that	Sie macht die Tür leise zu, damit das Keind nicht aufwacht.	She closes the door quietly, so that the child doesn't wake up.
als	when (past)	Als ich jünger war, hatte ich einen Hund und zwei Katzen.	When I was younger, I had a dog and two cats.
als ob, als	as if	Er hat mich angeschaut, als ob er mich niemals im Leben gesehen hätte.	He looked at me as if he had never seen me before in his life.
Seit / seitdem	since (time)	Ich habe ihn nur einmal gesehen, seitdem ich hier bin.	I've only see him once since I've been here.
sobald	as soon as	Ruf mich bitte an, sobald du zu Hause bist.	Please call me as soon as you're home.
Sodas	so that	Ich preßte mir die Hand auf den Mund, Sodas ich nicht lachen konnte.	I preßed my hand against my mouth so that I couldn't laugh.
solange	as long as	Solange die Sonne scheint, bin ich glücklich.	As long as the sun shines, I'm happy.
sooft	whenever	Ich besuche meine Oma, sooft ich kann.	I visit my grandmother whenever I can
um ... zu	in order to	Er macht das Licht an, um besser zu sehen.	He turns on the light in order to see better.
während	during, while, whereas	Nero spielte seine Flöte während Rom brannte.	Nero played his flute while Rome burned.
falls	in case, if	Hier ist meine Handynummer, falls ich mich verlaufe.	Here is my mobile number, in case I get lost.
indem	by ... -ing	Sie spart Geld, indem sie ihre Kleidung online kauft.	She saves money by buying her clothes online.
nachdem	after	Er kommt zu Besuch, nachdem er mit dem Studium fertig ist.	He's coming to visit after he's finished his studies.
bevor / ehe	before	Es gibt immer eine halbe Stunde Werbung, bevor der Film Beginnt.	There is always half an hour of advertisements before the film Begins.
bis	until, by (time)	Es daürt noch eine Stunde, bis ich fertig bin.	It'll be another hour until I'm finished.
da	as (because)	Er konnte das Geschenk nicht kaufen, da er nicht genug Geld hatte.	He couldn't buy the present, as he didn't have enough money.
damit	so that	Sie macht die Tür leise zu, damit das Keind nicht aufwacht.	She closes the door quietly, so that the child doesn't wake up.

See the table below and notice how the word order in both clauses remains the same in spite of the

Coordinating Conjunctions   O S U D A

O - ODER OR
S - SONDERN   BUT
U - UND AND
D - DENN BECAUSE
A - ABER BUT

Coordinating Conjunction	Meaning	Example	English
oder	or	Sollen wir ein Buch lesen oder (sollen wir) ein Bild malen?	Should we read a book or (should we) paint a picture?
sondern	(but) rather	Irland ist nicht ein großes Land, sondern (ist es) eine kleine Insel.	Ireland is not a big country, but rather (it is) a small island.
und	and	Ich spiele Gitarre und ich spiele auch Klavier.	I play guitar and I also play piano.
denn	because	Er möchte eine Banane essen, denn er hat Hunger.	He wants to eat a banana because he is hungry.
aber	but	Ich will ins Keino gehen aber ich bin zu faul.	I want to go to the cinema but I'm too lazy.
beziehungsweise	or more precisely	Er fliegt morgen nach Frankreich, bzw. er fliegt nach Paris.	Tomorrow he's flying to France, or more precisely, he's flying to Paris.

**Note: aber and jedoch can move around to change the emphasis of the clause:

jedoch	but, however	Alle wollten nach Hause, jedoch ich wollte weiter feiern.	Everyone wanted to go home, but I wanted to party on.
jedoch	but, however	Alle wollten nach Hause, ich jedoch wollte weiter feiern.	Everyone wanted to go home, I, however, wanted to party on.
jedoch	but, however	Alle wollten nach Hause, ich wollte jedoch weiter feiern.	Everyone wanted to go home, I wanted to party on, however.

Two-Part Coordinating Conjunctions

Occupy position 1 in a sentence, which means that the verb normally comes directly after the conjunction. An exception to this is the "oder" part of "entweder…oder", due to "oder" being a singular coordinating conjunction (see table above).
The normal sentence structure would be:

Einerseits mag ich Bücher, andererseits finde ich Filme toll.

[conjunction (1)] Verb (2) + Subject (3) + Object (4), [conjunction (1)] Verb (2) + Subject (3) + Object (4)

Have a look at the table below and notice how the word order in both clauses follows the same pattern. Pay particular attention to the conjunction in position 1:

Conjunctions	Meaning	Example	English
entweder ... oder	either ... or	Entweder gehen wir ins Keino oder wir gehen ins Museum.	Either we're going to the cinema or we're going to the museum.
weder ... noch	neither ... nor	Ich habe weder Brüder noch Schwestern.	I have neither brothers nor sisters.
sowohl ... als auch	both ... and	Er hat sowohl die Küche geputzt, als auch das Wohnzimmer aufgeräumt.	He both cleaned the kitchen and tidied the living room.
einerseits ... andererseits	on one hand ... on the other hand	Einerseits bin ich müde, andererseits kann ich nicht schlafen.	On the one hand I'm tired, on the other hand I can't sleep.
bald ... bald	sometimes ... sometimes	Bald Regnet es, bald scheint die Sonne.	Sometimes it rains, sometimes the sun shines.
mal ... mal	sometimes ... sometimes	Mal ist das Wetter furchtbar kalt, mal ist es richtig schön.	Sometimes the weather is terribly cold, sometimes it is very nice.
teils ... teils	partly ... partly	Das Museum ist teils langweilig, teils intereßant.	The museum is partly boring, partly interesting.
Just like in English, some conjunctions can be used in different positions for emphasis:			
entweder ... oder	either ... or	Entweder gehen wir ins Keino, oder wir gehen ins Museum.	Either we're going to the cinema or we're going to the museum.
entweder ... oder	either ... or	Wir gehen entweder ins Keindo, oder wir gehen ins Museum.	We're going to either the cinema, or to the museum.
einerseits ... andererseits	on the one hand ... on the other hand	Einerseits bin ich müde, andererseits kann ich nicht schlafen.	On the one hand I'm tired, on the other hand I can't sleep.
einerseits ... andererseits	on the one hand ... on the other hand	Ich bin einerseits müde, andererseits kann ich nicht schlafen.	I'm tired on the one hand, but on the other hand I can't sleep.

Besides, the above there are some prepositions, which behave like sub-ordinate or co-ordinate conjunctions. Please note that – A conjunction does not change the conjunction until it is specifically meant to change.

Um.. zu +Infinitiv – in order to (sub-ordinate)
E.g. Ich weiß, dass mein Freund fleißig ist
(conjunction – daß)

Ich lerne Spanisch, um gute Noten zu bekommen
(um..zu infinitiv)

Statt.. zu + Infinitiv – instead of (sub-ordinate)
Er fährt mit dem Bus, statt mit dem Auto zu fahren.

Stattdessen – instead of that (co-ordinate)

Er fährt nicht mit dem Auto. Er fa fährt ehrt mi dem Bus.
Er fährt nicht mit dem Auto stattdessen fährt er mit dem Bus.

Adjective and Endings

Adjective is word which tells the specialty of a noun or pronoun.
German language uses ENDINGS with adjectives according to the Gender, Number and Case.

Adjectives do not take an ending if it succeeds the NOUN ie. comes after the NOUN. Although the adjective is at the end of the Sentence but the noun has been skipped just to avoid the repetition, it will take an ENDING.
E.g., 1. Das Buch ist interessant.

In the sentence above, the adjective "INTERESSANT" has come after the noun and at the end of the sentence. So there will be no ENDING.

2. Welchen Kuli kaufst Du? Den blauen oder den schwarzen?
Had it been a full and complete answer with all the elements the question would have been:
Kaufst du den blauen oder den schwarzen Kuli?

Since "KULI" has already been come in the first sentence, in the second sentence, it has not been repeated. But this will not take away the right to use the adjective Ending.

There is a basic difference between the examples 1 and 2
In the 1st example, the sentence is complete. Neither anything has been added no anything has been skipped, whereas in the second example "KULI has been skipped which does not make any difference in the use of adjective endings.

There are three types of ADJECTIVE ENDINGS

With Definite Article   (Bestimmt)

With Indefinite Article   (Unbestimmt)

Without Article   (OHNE)

* there are a few more words which use adjective-ENDINGs. These are - ALLE, **KEINE**, EINIGE, WENIGE, ANDERE, Viele etc.
* Adjective -Endings will start with " - e" only

1. With Definite (Bestimmt) Article

Endings				
	MAS	NEU	FEM	PL
Nom	-e	-e	-e	-en
Akk	-en	-e	-e	-en
Dat	-en	-en	-en	-en
Gen	-en	-en	-en	-en

Same endings with dieser, jeder, welcher etc.

2. With Indefinite (Unbestimmt) Article

	MAS	NEU	FEM	PL
Nom	-er	-es	-e	-en
Akk	-en	-es	-e	-en
Dat	-en	-en	-en	-en
Gen	-en	-en	-en	-en

Same endings with all the possessive pronouns and **"KEINE"** the endings in plural is with possessive pronouns and

3. Without (OHNE) Article

	MAS	NEU	FEM	PL
Nom	-er	-es	-e	-e
Akk	-en	-es	-e	-e
Dat	-em	-em	r	-en
Gen	-en	-en	-er	-en

4. With other words

1   Alle -en
2   Wenige, einige, andere, mehrere, viele – e

There are a number of ways to understand Adjective endings so one does not need to learn it.

How to understand ?

1 With DEFINITE (BESTIMMT) article
   a   With all the three genders in Nominative case -e
   b   With NEU (NUTRAL) and FEM (FEMININE) genders in ACCUSATIVE case - e (no change in the form of definite article i.e. it remains as as is DAS and DIE with neutral and feminine genders
   c   Rest all - en
2   With INDEFINITE (UNBESTIMMT) article
   Has no plural, endings of plural is with Possessive Pronoun etc)

The ending of DEFINITE article becomes the
Adjective Endings with all the three genders in NOMINATIVE case
b   With neutral and FEMININE in ALL Cases - same as in Nominative case (same logic as in
         DEFINITE Article (Bestimmt)

3   Without Article
a   The ending of DEFINITE Article becomes the Akk Ending of Without (OHNE) Article
b   With MASCULINE and NEUTRAL in GENITIVE Case - en (exception

Clues

If the article or Possessive Pronoun is given, there are many Clue(s)s which can directly tell you the ADJECTIVE Ending:
a DEN, DEM, DES, EINEN, EINEM, EINER, EINER -en
b DAS, EINE (only Singular, U.A.) -e.
c DER - (a) If masculine -e   (b) if any other -en
d DIE - (a) if Feminine -e   (b) if plural   - en
e EIN - (a) If masculine - er (b) if neutral -es

One can also recognize the ending through following three steps
a See whether it is with Definite Article or Indefinite Articl
b Checkout the gender of the word for which adjective has been used
c Find out the case

Examples
1 Er kauft ein blaues Auto.   Analysis
Through Steps -   Unbestimmt Arti. - neu - Akku - es
                         (ein) Auto   (kaufen is akku)
Through Clue(s)s -   ein - Auto is neu - Akkusativ - es
                         Sie kauft einen neuen Kuli.

Analysis
Through Steps -   Unbestimmt Arti.- mas - Akk - en
                         einen   -r Kuli   kaufe -akkusativ
Through Clue(s)s -   einen   en
                         Das kleine Kid geht mit seiner alten Mutter.

Analysis
Through Steps -   a. Bestimmt Article - neu Nominativ -
                         (das)   - s Keind   - Subject
                         b. unbestimmt Artikel - Fem - Dat - en
                         seiner   -e Mutter   mit - takes Dattiv

Personal Pronom.
Through Clue(s)s -   a. - das   -e
                         b. - seiner (einer) -en
4 Junge Leute helfen alten Leuten.
Through Steps -   "a. Ohne Artikel (O.A.)-   plural - Dat - en
                         (no article)   (-e Leute)   - (Sub) "
                         b. Ohne Artikel (O.A.)-   plural - Dat - en
                         "c. Ohne Artikel -   plural - Dat - en
(no article) (Leute) verb -   Helfen takes Dattiv"
Through Clue(s)s -   a. No Clue(s)s
                         b. No Clue(s)s
                         c. No Clue(s)s

In case OA (Ohne Artikel) one has to go through steps only, as there I no clue.

Additional 100 Verbs for Beginners

Auxiliary verbs x form, they are mostly used in Simple Past.

1. **sein (war - ist gewesen) - to be**
   Ich bin müde *(I am tired)*. Sie war gestern nicht da *(She was not there yesterday)*.
   Warst du schon in Deutschland *(Have you been to Germany)*?

2. **haben (hatte - hat gehabt) - to have**
   Hast du Geschwister *(Do you have siblings)*?
   Ich hatte **keine** Zeit *(I had no time)*.

3. **werden (wurde - ist geworden) - to become, to get**
   Es wird gut *(It will be fine)*. Sie ist Lehrerin geworden *(She has become a teacher)*.
   Ich will Schauspielerin werden *(I want to become an actreß)*.

Modal Verbes

4. **können (konnte) - to be able, to know**
   Ich kann nicht schwimmen *(I can't swim)*.
   Wir können am Samstag nicht kommen *(We can't come on Saturday)*.

5. **müssen (mußte) - to have to, need**
   Ich muß nach Hause gehen *(I have to go home)*.
   Er mußte gestern arbeiten *(He had to work yesterday)*.

6. **wollen (wollte) - to want**
   Sie will dich nicht sehen *(She doesn't want to see you)*.
   Ich wollte das Buch zu Ende lesen *(I wanted to finish the book)*.

7. **sollen (sollte) - to be supposed to, ought to, should**
   Was soll ich machen *(What should I do)*?
   Du sollst nicht lügen *(You should not lie)*.

8. **dürfen (durfte) - to be allowed, may, can**
   Darf ich auf dem Balkon grillen *(May I have a barbecü on the balcony)*?
   Hier darf man nicht rauchen *(You are not allowed to smoke here)*.

9. **mögen (mochte) - to like, want**
   Ich mag Pizza *(I like Pizza)*. Alle mögen ihn *(Everybody likes him)*.

10. **möchten - to wish (this is a form of the verb mögen)**
   Möchten Sie etwas trinken *(Would you like to drink something)*?
   Ich möchte etwas fragen *(I would like to ask something)*.

Regular verbs
The following verbs have a **Reg**ular conjugation pattern in the present tense and you can see the past participle
form in the brackets. Some of them are also used in Simple Past in spoken German, so I included this form too.

11. **gehen (ist gegangen) - to go, walk**
   Ich gehe nach Hause *(I'm going home)*.
   Wir sind gestern ins Theater ge.gangen *(We went to the theater yesterday)*.

12. **kommen (ist gekommen) - to come**
   Wann kommst du zurück *(When are you coming back)*?
   Ich bin gestern um 22.00 Uhr gekommen *(I came at 22.00 yesterday)*.

13. **reisen (ist gereist) - to travel**
   Ich reise gern *(I like to travel)*. I
   ch bin nach Deutschland gereist *(I traveled to Germany)*.

14. **fliegen (ist geflogen) - to fly**
   Meine Mutter fliegt nicht gerne *(My mother doesn't like flying)*.
   Sie ist mit dem Flugzeug nach Deutschland geflogen *(She flew to Germany by plane)*.

15. **wohnen (hat gewohnt) - to live**
   Wo wohnst du *(Where do you live)*?
   Ich habe 2 Jahre in Deutschland gewohnt *(I lived in Germany for 2 years)*.

16. **heißen (hieß - hat geheißen) - to be called, to mean**
   Wie heißt du *(What is your name)*?
   Wir heißen Anna und Clara *(We are Anna and Clara)*.

17. **kaufen (hat gekauft) - to buy**
   Er kauft Brot in der Bäckerei *(He buys bread in the bakery)*.
   Ich habe gestern ein neüs Kleid gekauft *(Yesterday I bought a new dreß)*.

18. **trinken (hat getrunken) - to drink**
   Was trinkst du gern *(What do you like to drink)*?
   Ich habe eine Tasse Kaffee getrunken *(I drank a cup of coffee)*.

19. **arbeiten (hat gearbeitet) - to work**
   Sie arbeiten von Montag bis Freitag *(They work from Monday to Friday)*.
   Wir haben gestern viel gearbeitet *(We worked a lot yesterday)*.

20. **machen (hat gemacht) - to make, do**
   Was machen Sie gerne *(What do you like to do)*?
   Was habt ihr gestern gemacht *(What did you do yesterday)*?

21. **fragen (hat gefragt) - to ask**
   Warum fragst du sie nicht *(Why don't you ask her)*?
   Ich habe meine Chefin gefragt *(I asked my boss)*.

22. **antworten (hat geantwortet) - to answer**
   Sie antwortet nicht *(She doesn't answer)*.
   Sie hat noch nicht geantwortet *(She has not answered yet)*.

23. **hören (hat gehört) - to hear, listen**
   Ich höre gerne Musik *(I like to listen to music)*.
   Habt ihr das neue Lied von Mark Forster gehört *(Did you hear the new song by Max Forster)*?

24. **sagen (hat gesagt) - to say, tell**
   Wir sagen die Wahrheit *(We are telling the truth)*.
   Was hat die Lehrerin gesagt *(What did the teacher say)*?

25. **verstehen (hat verstanden) - to understand**
   Ich verstehe die Frage nicht *(I don't understand the qüstion)*.
   Hast du alles richtig verstanden *(Did you understand everything correctly)*?

26. **denken (dachte - hat gedacht) - to think**

Was denkst du daran *(What do you think of that)*?
Ich dachte, du kommst aus den USA *(I thought you were from the USA)*.

27. suchen (hat gesucht) - to search, look for
Ich suche eine neue Wohnung *(I am lookeing for a new apartment)*.
Ich habe ein Geschenk gesucht *(I was lookeing for a gift)*.

28. finden (hat gefunden) - to find, think
Wie findest du diese Tasche *(How do you like(find) this bag)*?
Sie hat einen Fehler im Text gefunden *(She found a mistake in the text)*.

29. bleiben (ist geblieben) - to stay
Ich bleibe morgen zu Hause *(I'll stay home tomorrow)*.
Warum bist du am Wochenende zu Hause geblieben *(Why did you stay home for the weekend)*?

30. bringen (hat gebracht) - to bring, take
Der Kellner bringt die Speisekarte *(The waiter brings the menu)*.
Ich habe meine Tochter zur Schule gebracht *(I took my daughter to school)*.

31. bedeuten (hat bedeutet) - to mean
Was bedeutet dieses Wort *(What does this word mean)*?
Was bedeutet Glück für dich *(What is happineß to you)*?

32. besuchen (besuchte - hat besucht) - to visit
Ich besuche meine Familie jeden Monat *(I visit my family every month)*.
Wir haben unsere Großeltern besucht *(We visited our grandparents)*.

33. schmecken (hat geschmeckt) - to taste
Das schmeckt gut *(It tastes good)*.
Hat Ihnen das Essen geschmeckt *(Did you like the food)*?

34. schreiben (hat geschrieben) - to write
Ich schreibe einen Brief *(I write a letter)*.
Wer hat dieses Buch geschrieben *(Who wrote this book)*?

35. spielen (hat gespielt) - to play
Spielst du Klavier *(Do you play the piano)*?
Wir haben gestern Fußball gespielt *(We played football yesterday)*.

36. lernen (hat gelernt) - to learn, study
Ihr lernt Deutsch *(You learn German)*.
Wo hast du Deutsch gelernt *(Where did you learn German)*?

37. zeigen (hat gezeigt) - to show
Ich will dir etwas zeigen *(I want to show you something)*.
Er hat uns seine Fotos gezeigt *(He showed us his photos)*.

38. kochen (hat gekocht) - to cook
Meine Mutter kocht gerne *(My mother likes to cook)*.
Sie hat Suppe gekocht *(She cooked soup)*.

39. Beginnen (hat Begonnen) - to Begin, start
Wann Beginnt der Unterricht *(When does the claß start)*?
Der Unterricht hat schon Begonnen *(The claß has already started)*.

40. stehen (hat gestanden) - to stand, be
Er steht im Stau *(He is stuck in traffic)*.
Wir haben lange in der Schlange gestanden *(We stood in line for a long time)*.

41. liegen (hat gele.gen) - to lie, be located
Das Handy liegt auf dem Tisch *(The phone is on the table)*.
Die Touristen liegen am Strand *(The tourists lay on the beach)*.

42. glauben (hat ge.glaubt) - to believe, think
Ich glaube dir *(I believe you)*.
Warum hast du mir nicht ge.glaubt *(Why didn't you believe me)*?

43. nennen (hat genannt) - to call, name
Man nennt junge Hunde Welpen *(Young dogs are called puppies)*.
Wir haben unseren Hund Charlie genannt *(We named our dog Charlie)*.

44. kennen (hat gekannt) - to know

Kennst du Peter *(Do you know Peter)*?
Ich kenne niemanden in dieser Stadt *(I don't know anyone in this city)*.

45. **stellen (hat gestellt) - to put, place**
Ich stelle die Vase auf den Tisch *(I put the vase on the table)*.
Wohin hast du die Vase gestellt *(Where did you put the vase)*?

46. **bekommen (hat bekommen) - to get, receive**
Ich bekomme immer viele Geschenke zum Geburtstag *(I always get many birthday presents)*. Wir haben noch **keine** Antwort bekommen *(We didn't receive an answer yet)*.

47. **bestellen (hat bestellt) - to order**
Wir bestellen Pizza *(We order pizza)*.
Ich habe ein Buch auf Amazon bestellt *(I ordered a book on Amazon)*.

48. **erzählen (hat erzählt) - to tell**
Er erzählt immer die gleiche Geschichte *(He always tells the same story)*.
Paul hat über seine Reise nach Japan erzählt *(Paul has told about his trip to Japan)*.

49. **versuchen (hat versucht) - to try, attempt**
Ich versuche, jeden Tag Deutsch zu lernen *(I try to learn German every day)*.
Wir haben alles versucht *(We have tried everything)*.

50. **erklären (hat erklärt) - to explain**
Die Lehrerin erklärt Grammatik *(The teacher explains grammar)*.
Er hat uns die Spiel**Regel**n erklärt *(He explained us the game rules)*.

51. **sitzen (hat gesessen) - to sit, be**
Das Keind will nicht im Keinderwagen sitzen *(The child does not want to sit in the stroller)*.
Sie sitzt am Fenster und liest *(She sits at the window and reads)*.

52. **gehören (gehörte - hat gehört) - to belong to**
Wem gehört dieses Buch *(Whose book is this)*?
Seit 1957 gehört das Saarland zur Bundesrepublik Deutschland *(Since 1957, the Saarland belongs to Germany)*.

53. **warten (hat gewartet) - to wait**
Wir warten auf dich *(We are waiting for you)*.
Habt ihr lange gewartet *(Did you wait a long time)*?

54. **erwarten (hat erwartet) - to expect**
Was erwartest du vom Leben in Deutschland *(What do you expect from life in Germany)*? Das habe ich nicht erwartet *(I did not expect that)*.

55. **verlieren (hat verloren) - to lose**
Sie verliert oft die Autoschlüssel *(She often loses the car keys)*.
Ich habe mein Handy verloren *(I've lost my mobile phone)*.

56. **le.gen (hat gele.gt) - to put, place**
Clara liegt das Buch auf den Tisch *(Clara puts the book on the table)*.
Sie hat die Tasche auf den Boden gele.gt *(She put the bag on the floor)*.

57. **Schließen (hat geschlossen) - to close, lock**
Anna schließt das Fenster *(Anna closes the window)*.
Er hat die Tür geschlossen *(He closed the door)*.

58. **öffnen (hat geöffnet) - to open**
Peter öffnet die Tür *(Peter opens the door)*.
Das Mädchen hat die Augen geöffnet *(The girl has opened her eyes)*.

59. **studieren (hat studiert) - to study**
Er studiert an der Universität Wien *(He studies at the University of Vienna)*.
Was hast du studiert *(What did you study)*?

60. **fehlen (hat gefehlt) - to miß, lack, be absent**
Meine Familie fehlt mir sehr *(I miß my family very much)*.
Wer fehlt heute *(Who is absent today)*?

61. **vergleichen (hat verglichen) - to compare**
Wir vergleichen die Preise in Deutschland und in der Schweiz *(We compare the prices in Germany and in Switzerland)*.

Warum vergleichst du dich immer mit anderen Menschen *(Why do you always compare yourself with other people)*?

62. **singen (hat gesungen) - to sing**
Ich singe nicht gern *(I don't like to sing)*.
Wer hat dieses Lied gesungen *(Who sung this song)*?

63. **tanzen (hat getanzt) - to dance**
Sie tanzt Salsa *(She dances salsa)*.
Wir haben die ganze Nacht lang getanzt *(We danced all night long)*.

64. **bezahlen (hat bezahlt) - to pay**
Er bezahlt die Rechnung *(He pays the bill)*.
Hast du deine Rechnungen schon bezahlt *(Have you already paid your bills)*?

65. **verdienen (hat verdient) - to earn, deserve**
Tom verdient viel Geld *(Tom earns a lot of money)*.
Du hast etwas Besseres verdient *(You deserve something better)*.

66. **reden (hat geredet) - to talk, speak**
Sie redet mit der Lehrerin *(He talks to the teacher)*.
Ich habe mit meiner Mutter geredet *(I talked to my mother)*.

67. **brauchen (brauchte - hat gebraucht) - to need**
Ich brauche mehr Zeit *(I need more time)*.
Brauchen Sie Hilfe *(Do you need help)*?

68. **passieren (ist passiert) - to happen**
Das passiert manchmal *(That happens sometimes)*.
Was ist gestern passiert *(What happened yesterday)*?

69. **kosten (hat gekostet) - to cost**
Wie viel kostet 1 kg Tomaten *(How much does 1 kg of tomatoes cost)*?
Wieviel hat dein Auto gekostet *(How much did you car cost)*?

70. **senden (hat gesendet/gesandt) - to send, post**
Ich sende dir ein SMS *(I will send you a text meßage)*.
Er hat die Rechnung per E-Mail gesendet *(He sent the bill by email)*.

71. **schicken (hat geschickt) - to send**
Er schickt eine Postkarte *(He sends a postcard)*.
Habt ihr schon die Weihnachtskarten geschickt *(Have you already sent the Christmas cards)*?

72. **heiraten (hat geheiratet) - to marry, get married**
Wir heiraten Ende Juni *(We marry at the end of June)*.
Sie haben in der Schweiz geheiratet *(They got married in Switzerland)*.

73. **sterben (ist gestorben) - to die**
Alle sterben früher oder später *(Everyone dies sooner or later)*.
Er ist vor 10 Jahren gestorben *(He died 10 years ago)*.

74. **feiern (hat gefeiert) - to celebrate**
Wir feiern immer zusammen Weihnachten *(We always celebrate Christmas together)*.
Warum hast du deinen Geburtstag nicht gefeiert *(Why didn't you celebrate your birthday)*?

75. **lieben (hat geliebt) - to love**
Ich liebe dich *(I love you)*.
Liebst du mich *(Do you love me)*?

76. **wiederholen (hat wiederholt) - to repeat, revise**
Können Sie bitte wiederholen *(Can you please repeat)*?
Ich habe alle Wörter vor dem Test wiederholt *(I revised all the words before the test)*.

77. teilen (hat geteilt) - to share
Ich teile deine Meinung nicht *(I don't share your opinion)*. Wir haben uns den Kuchen geteilt *(We shared the cake)*.

Stem-changing verbs
Stem-changing verbs change the vowel in second and third person singular in the present tense.

78. wissen (wußte - hat gewußt) - to know
Das weiß ich leider nicht *(Unfortunately I do not know it)*.
Er wußte das auch nicht *(He didn't know that either)*.

79. fahren (ist gefahren) - to drive, go
Er fährt zur Arbeit mit dem Bus *(He goes to work by bus)*.
Wir sind am Wochenende nach München gefahren *(We went to Munich at the weekend)*.

80. essen (hat ge.gessen) - to eat
Mein Sohn ißt jeden Tag Schokolade *(My son eats chocolate every day)*.
Hast du schon etwas ge.gessen *(Did you eat something)*?

81.schlafen (hat geschlafen) - to sleep
Hast du gut geschlafen *(Did you sleep well)*?
Ich habe nicht genug geschlafen *(I did not sleep enough)*.

82. geben (hat ge.geben) - to give
Laura gibt mir das Buch *(Laura gives me the book)*.
Wir haben Anna die Schlüßel ge.geben *(We gave Anna the keys)*.

83. sehen (hat gesehen) - to see
Siehst du den Hund da *(Do you see the dog there)*?
Sie hat noch nie eine Giraffe gesehen *(She has never seen a giraffe)*.

84. sprechen (hat gesprochen) - to speak
Anna spricht zu schnell *(Anna speaks too fast)*.
Wann hast du mit Paul gesprochen *(When did you talk to Paul)*?

85. nehmen (hat genommen) - to take
Er nimmt den falschen Bus *(He takes the wrong bus)*.
Ich habe Urlaub genommen *(I took a vacation)*.

86. lesen (hat gelesen) - to read
Liest du gerne Bücher *(Do you like reading books)*?
Ich habe dieses Buch noch nicht gelesen *(I haven't read this book yet)*.

87. vergessen (hat vergessen) - to forget
Sie vergißt immer ihre Schlüssel *(She always forgets her keys)*.
Hast du etwas vergessen *(Did you forget something)*?

88. waschen (hat gewaschen) - to wash
Wie oft wäschst du deine Jeans *(How often do you wash your jeans)*?
Ich habe meine Haare gewaschen *(I have washed my hair)*.

89. laufen (ist gelaufen) - to run, walk
Die Frau läuft über die Straße *(The woman is walkeing acroß the street)*.
Er ist 5 Kilometer gelaufen *(He has run 5 kilometers)*.

90. tragen (hat getragen) - to wear, carry
Maria trägt gerne Kleider *(Maria likes to wear dresses)*.
Ich habe gestern ein weißes Kleid getragen *(Yesterday I wore a white dress)*.

Verbs with separable prefixes
In the present tense, the prefixes of the following verbs are separated and put at the end of the sentence.

91. aussehen (hat ausgesehen) - to look (appear)
Du siehst immer gut aus *(You always look good)*.
Wie hat sie ausgesehen *(How did she look like)*?

92. anfangen (hat angefangen) - to start, Begin
Der Unterricht fängt um 12.00 Uhr an *(Claßes start at 12.00)*.
Wir haben noch nicht angefangen *(We have not started yet)*.

93. anrufen (hat angerufen) - to call
Ich rufe meine Oma an *(I call my grandma)*.
Sie hat mich gestern angerufen *(She called me yesterday)*.

94. aufstehen (ist aufgestanden) - to get up, stand up
Wann stehst du normalerweise auf *(When do you usually get up)*?
Ich bin heute um 6.00 Uhr aufgestanden *(I got up at 6:00 today)*.

95. einladen (hat eingeladen) - to invite

Ich lade dich zum Essen ein *(I invite you for dinner)*.
Sie hat viele Freunde zur Geburtstagsparty eingeladen *(She has invited many friends to the birthday party)*.

Reflexive verbs

Some of these verbs can be used with or without the reflexive pronoun "sich".

96. **(sich) fühlen (hat gefühlt) - to feel**
Ich fühle mich schuldig *(I feel guilty)*.
Wie fühlen sich Migranten in Deutschland *(How do migrants feel in Germany)*?

97. **interessieren (hat interessiert) - to interest sich interessieren (hat sich interessiert) für etwas - to be interested in something**
Sie interessiert sich für Kunst *(She is interested in art)*.
Ich habe mich schon immer für Fremdsprachen intereßiert *(I have always been interested in foreign languages)*.

98. **erinnern (hat erinnert) - to remind sich erinnern (hat erinnert) an etwas - to remember something**
Maria erinnert sich an ihre Keindheit in Spanien *(Maria remembers her childhood in Spain)*. Facebook hat mich an seinen Geburtstag erinnert *(Facebook reminded me of his birthday)*.

99. **treffen (hat getroffen) - to meet sich treffen (hat getroffen) - to meet up**
Paul trifft seine Freunde am Wochenende *(Paul meets his friends on the weekend)*.
Ich habe ihn gestern getroffen *(I met him yesterday)*.

100. **(sich) vorstellen (hat vorgestellt) - to imagine, to introduce**
Ich kann mir das Leben ohne Handy nicht vorstellen *(I can't imagine life without a mobile phone)*.
Ich habe mir Deutschland anders vorgestellt *(I imagined Germany differently)*.

Days of the week in German **der Tag, -e** – day(s)

der Montag – Monday	**am Montag** – on Monday	**Montags** – on Mondays
der Dienstag – Tuesday	**am Dienstag** – on Tüsday	**Dienstags** – on Tuesdays
der Mittwoch – Wednesday	**am Mittwoch** – on Wednesday	**Mittwochs** – on Wednesdays
der Donnerstag – Thursday	**am Donnerstag** – on Thursday	**Donnerstags** – on Thursdays
der Freitag – Friday	**am Freitag** – on Friday	**Freitags** – on Fridays
der Samstag – Saturday	**am Samstag** – on Saturday	**Samstags** – on Saturdays
der Sonntag – Sunday	**am Sonntag** – on Sunday	**sonntags** – on Sundays
das Wochenende – weekend	**am Wochenende** – on the weekend	wochenends(this words exists, but is rarely used)

The months in German are very similar to English but you need to be careful with pronunciation. Even if the months are written the same, German pronunciation will be different.

The Months in German **der Monat, -e** – the month(s)

der Januar – January	**im Januar – in January**
der Februar – February	**im Februar – in February**
der März – March	**im März – in March**
der April – April	**im April – in April**
der Mai – May	**im Mai – in May**
der Juni – June	**im Juni – in June**
der Juli – July	**im Juli – in July**
der August – August	**im August – in August**
der September – September	**im September – in September**
der Oktober – October	**im Oktober – in October**
der November – November	**im November – in November**
der Dezember – December	**im Dezember – in December**

Seasons in German **die Jahreszeit, -en** – season(s)

der Winter – winter	**im Winter – in winter**
der Frühling – spring	**im Frühling – in spring**
der Sommer – summer	**im Sommer – in summer**
der Herbst – autumn/fall	**im Herbst – in autumn/fall**

- *Was ist deine Lieblingsjahreszeit? (What is your favorite season?)*
- *In welchem Monat hast du Geburtstag? (In which month is your birthday)?*
- *Welcher Tag ist heute? (What day is today)?*

Reflexive verbs in Accusative

Verb	Translation	Example
sich die Haare bürsten	brush something	Du bürstest dir die Haare.
sich die Haare kämmen	comb hairs	Ich habe mir die Haare gekämmt.
sich etwas anziehen	put something on	Ich ziehe mir eine Jacke an.
sich etwas ausziehen	take something off	Du ziehst dir die Schuhe aus.
sich etwas putzen	clean something	Ich putze mir jeden Morgen und Abend die Zähne.
sich wehtun	hurt yourself	Hast du dir wehgetan?

Levels A1 + A2

Verb	Translation	Example
sich duschen	shower	Ich dusche mich.
sich waschen	wash oneself	Du wäschst dich.
sich anziehen	get dreßed/dreß oneself	Ich stehe auf und ziehe mich an.
sich ausziehen	undreß oneself	Er zieht sich aus und geht ins Bett.
sich baden	bath oneself	Sonntags bade ich mich.
sich befinden	be/be located	Das Brandenburger Tor befindet sich in Berlin.
sich beschweren (über)	complain	Die Schüler beschweren sich über den schweren Test.
sich freuen	look forward to/be glad about	Wir freuen uns auf die Ferien.
sich fühlen	feel	Wie geht es dir? Fühlst du dich heute besser?
sich informieren	inform oneself	Sie informieren sich über die Sehenswürdigkiten der Stadt.
sich interessieren	be interested in	Interessiert ihr euch für Geschichte?
sich kämmen	comb	Kämm dich bitte! Deine Haare sind ganz zerzaust.
sich legen	lie	Wollen wir uns an den Strand legen?
sich rasieren	shave	Mein Vater rasiert sich nicht mehr.
sich setzen	sit	Setzen Sie sich, bitte!
sich stellen	stand	Er stellt sich auf den Stuhl, dann kann ihn jeder sehen.
sich treffen	meet	Triffst du dich morgen mit Beate?
sich verletzen	injure oneself	Ich bin vom Rad gestürzt und habe mich verletzt.
sich verabschieden	say goodbye	Wir müssen uns leider schon verabschieden.
sich vorstellen	introduce oneself	Ich möchte mich kurz vorstellen. Ich heiße Erwin Müller und komme aus München.

Reflexive Verbs in Dative

Verb	Translation	Example
sich die Haare bürsten	brush something	Du bürstest dir die Haare.
sich die Haare kämmen	comb something	Ich habe mir die Haare gekämmt.
sich etwas anziehen	put something on	Ich ziehe mir eine Jacke an.
sich etwas ausziehen	take something off	Du ziehst dir die Schuhe aus.
sich etwas putzen	clean something	Ich putze mir jeden Morgen und Abend die Zähne.
sich wehtun	hurt yourself	Hast du dir wehgetan?
sich die Haare bürsten	brush something	Du bürstest dir die Haare.
sich die Haare kämmen	comb something	Ich habe mir die Haare gekämmt.
sich etwas anziehen	put something on	Ich ziehe mir eine Jacke an.
sich etwas ausziehen	take something off	Du ziehst dir die Schuhe aus.
sich etwas putzen	clean something	Ich putze mir jeden Morgen und Abend die Zähne.
sich wehtun	hurt yourself	Hast du dir wehgetan?

Level B1

Reflexive verbs in accusative

Verb	Translation	Example
sich ändern	change	Die Zeiten haben sich geändert.
sich anmelden	Register	Wo kann man sich für den Kurs anmelden?
sich anschauen	look at oneself	Schau dich mal im Spiegel an! Du bist ganz schmutzig im Gesicht.
sich anschnallen	fasten	Schnallen Sie sich während der Fahrt bitte an!
sich ärgern	be annoyed	Er ärgerte sich über seinen Fehler.
sich bedanken	thank	Ich möchte mich bei dir für das schöne Geschenk bedanken.
sich beeilen	hurry	Wir müssen uns beeilen, sonst verpassen wir den Zug.
sich beWegen	move/exercise	Sei nicht so faul! Du mußt dich mehr beWegen!

sich bewerben	apply	Karin hat sich bei der Touristinformation beworben.
sich entscheiden	decide	Ich kann mich nicht entscheiden, was ich essen soll. Es sieht alles lecker aus.
sich entschuldigen	Apologize /excuse	Bitte entschuldigen Sie mich einen Moment. Ich muß ans Telefon gehen.
sich erholen	relax/rest	Hast du dich im Urlaub gut erholt?
sich hinlegen	lie down	Mir geht es nicht gut. Ich werde mich ein paar Minuten hinlegen.
	lay something down	
sich hinsetzen	sit down	Du mußt nicht stehen, du darfst dich gern hinsetzen.
sich irren	be wrong/mistaken	Du irrst dich, München ist nicht die Hauptstadt von Deutschland. {{info::You are mistaken, Munich is not the capital of Germany. Literally: You are wrong/mistake yourself.)
sich konzentrieren	concentrate	Keinder, seid leise! Ich muß mich konzentrieren.
sich trennen (von)	break up with/separate from	Lina hat sich von ihrem Freund getrennt.
sich verirren	get lost/lose one's way	Wir haben uns im Wald verirrt.
sich verlieben	fall in love	Hast du dich im Urlaub verliebt?
sich wohlfühlen	feel good	Du hast eine schöne Wohnung. Da kann man sich richtig wohlfühlen.

Reflexive verbs in dativ

Verb	**Translation**	**Example**
sich etwas überlegen	think about something	Ich werde mir eine Lösung überlegen.
sich etwas vorstellen	imagine something	Kannst du dir vorstellen, was gestern passiert ist?
sich etwas wünschen	wish for something	Was wünschst du dir zum Geburtstag?

Level B2
Reflexive verbs in accusative

Verb	Translation	Example
sich amüsieren	enjoy oneself	Wir haben uns auf der Party prächtig amüsiert.
sich anfühlen	feel	Das Material fühlt sich sehr weich an.
sich auf**Regen**	work oneself up	**Reg** dich nicht über die Fehler der anderen auf! Du bist selbst nicht perfekt.
sich auskennen	be well informed/to know one's way around something	Ich kenne mich in dieser Gegend gar nicht aus.
sich ausruhen	take/have a rest	Nach der langen Fahrt möchtest du dich sicher etwas ausruhen.
sich ausweisen	identify oneself/provide identification	Können Sie sich irgendwie ausweisen?
sich bedienen	help oneself	Das Essen steht auf dem Tisch in der Küche. Bedient euch einfach!
sich beruhigen	calm oneself	Beruhige dich wieder! Es ist alles nicht so schlimm.
sich beschäftigen (mit)	deal with/busy oneself with	In dieser Lektion beschäftigen wir uns mit reflexiven Verben.
sich einschreiben	**Register**/enrol	Warum habt ihr euch nicht für den Fortgeschrittenen-Kurs eingeschrieben?
sich entschließen	decide	Mein Sohn hat sich entschlossen, Astronaut zu werden.
sich entwickeln	develop/evolve/grow	Laß uns abwarten, wie sich die Situation entwickelt.
sich erkälten	catch a cold	Carla hat sich im Urlaub erkältet.
sich erkundigen	find out	Ich werde mich erkundigen, von welchem Gleis unser Zug abfährt.
sich fortbilden	further/continü one's education	An der Volkshochschule kann man sich auf verschiedenen Gebieten fortbilden.
sich fragen	ask yourself/wonder	Ich frage mich, woher du das alles weißt.
sich fürchten	be afraid	Unsere Katze fürchtet sich vor fremden Leuten.
sich langweilen	feel/get/be bored	Sie hat so ein interessantes Leben, sie hat sich noch nie gelangweilt.
sich melden	answer/report/**Register**	Karl ist so schüchtern – er meldet sich im Unterricht nie.
sich scheiden lassen	divorce	Frau Lehmann will sich (von ihrem Mann) scheiden lassen.
sich täuschen	make a mistake/be mistaken	Du hast Recht, ich habe mich getäuscht.
sich übergeben	vomit	Plötzlich wurde mir so schlecht, dass ich mich übergeben mußte.
sich verabreden	make an appointment/arrangement/date	Du bist so ele.gant gekleidet. Hast du dich mit jemandem verabredet?
sich verändern	change	Seit unserem letzten Besuch hat sich die Stadt sehr verändert.
sich verfahren	lose one's way/ get lost	Ich weiß nicht, wo wir sind. Ich glaube, wir haben uns verfahren.
sich verlassen (auf)	rely on/trust in	Kann ich mich darauf verlassen, daß ihr Brot mitbringt?
sich verstecken	hide	Der Junge versteckt sich immer hinter der Tür und erschreckt seine Schwester.
sich verteidigen	defend oneself	Wir lernen Karate, um uns im Notfall verteidigen zu können.
sich weiterbilden	further/continü one's education	Wenn du in deinem Job gut sein willst, mußt du dich ständig weiterbilden.
sich wundern	wonder/be surprised	Sie wundern sich, warum wir so fröhlich sind.
sich vorbereiten	prepare (oneself)	Habt ihr euch gut auf die Prüfung vorbereitet?

Reflexive Verbs in Dative

Verb	Translation	Example
sich etwas leisten	afford somethine	So ein teures Auto kann ich mir nicht leisten.
sich Zeit nehmen	take time for oneself	Ich nehme mir morgen Zeit und gehe mit dir ins Kino.
sich Zeit lassen	take one's time	Lass dir Zeit, es eilt nicht.

Level C1
Reflexive Verbs in accusative

Verb	Translation	Example
sich beherrschen	control/restrain oneself	Wenn ich das Lied höre, muss ich tanzen. Da kann ich mich nicht beherrschen.
sich einsetzen	campaign	Der Schauspieler setzt sich sehr für die Umwelt ein.
sich ereignen	occur/take place/happen	Seit letzter Woche hat sich nichts Besonderes ereignet.
sich gedulden	be patient/ bear with somebody	Bitte gedulden Sie sich noch einen Moment. Ich habe gleich für Sie Zeit.
sich schämen	feel ashamed/be embarrassed	Für dein Verhalten musst du dich nicht schämen.

sich sehnen (nach)	yearn/crave	Bei dem grauen Wetter sehne ich mich nach Sonne und Palmen.
sich trauen	dare/have the courage to do something	Ich traute mich nicht, ihr meine Meinung zu sagen.

Separable verbs (Trennbare Verben) and inseparable verbs (Untrennbare Verben) in German are verbs whose meaning is altered by the addition of a prefix. Prefixes that are separable are separated from their verb in the conjugated form

e.g. anstehen – ich stehe an (to que – I que).

Whereas, inseparable prefixes cannot be separated from their verb e.g. bestehen
– du bestehest (to pass – you Pass).

The prefix determines whether a verb is separable or not.

List of Separable Verbs

The verbs with the following prefixes are separable:
ab-, an-, auf-, aus-, bei-, ein-, los-, mit-, nach-,
her-, hin-, vor-, Weg-, zu-, zurück-

In the finite Form, these verbs are separated from their prefix, which usually comes at the end of the sentence.
Example:
Ich stehe an der Kasse an.

In the past participle, we add ge- between the prefix and the verb.
Example:
Ich habe an der Kasse angestanden.

List of Inseparable Verbs
Verbs with the following prefixes are inseparable:
be-, emp-, ent-, er-, ge-, misse-, ver-, zer-

These prefixes remain a permanent part of the verb, even in the finite form.
Example: Ich bestehe die Prüfung.

The past participle of inseparable verbs is not formed with ge.
Example: Ich habe die Prüfung bestanden.

German Verbs Separable and / or Inseparable both
The verbs with the following prefixes can be either separable or inseparable:

durch-, hinter-, über-, um-, unter-
Some verbs with these prefixes are always separable.
Example: umschauen – er schaut sich um

Some other verbs with these prefixes are never separable.
Example: umarmen – sie umarmt ihn

Some verbs with these prefixes can be either separable or inseparable. In this case, the separable verb and the inseparable verb have two different meanings.
Example: umfahren (knock-down)   - Er umfährt das Schild. Example   Er fährt das Schild um. (go around)   - Er umfährt das Schild.

separable verbs		
prefix	examples	translation
ab	abholen	pick up
	abheben	take off
an	anfangen	Begin
	anrufen	call, phone

auf	aufhören	stop
	aufstehen	get up
aus	ausgehen	go out
	aussehen	look, appear
bei	beibringen	teach
	beitreten	join
ein	einkaufen	shop
	einschlafen	fall asleep
fern	fernsehen	watch tv
fort	fortgehen	go away
	fortsetzen	continue
her	herkommen	come from
	herstellen	manufacture
hin	hinfahren	drive there
	hinstellen	place
los	losfahren	drive off
	loswerden	get rid off
mit	mitbringen	bring along
	mitnehmen	take along
nach	nachdenken	think
	nachfragen	ask after
statt	stattfinden	take place
	stattgeben	grant
vor	vorhaben	have planned
	vorstellen	imagine
vorbei	vorbeikommen	come by
Weg	Weggehen	go away
	Wegnehmen	take away
zu	zuhören	listen
	zugeben	admite
zurück	zurückgeben	give back
	zurückkommen	come back
zusammen	zusammenfassen	summarize
	zusammenkommen	come together
Further prefixes (seldom used):		
da, dabei, daran, empor, entgegen,		
entlang, fehl, fest, gegenüber, gleich,		
herauf, heraus, hinweg, hinzu, zurecht, zwischen		

Inseparable verbs		
prefix	examples	translation
ant	antworten	answer
be	bekommen	get
	besuchen	visit
emp	empfangen	receive
	empfehlen	recommend
ent	entdecken	discover
	entfernen	remove
er	erkennen	recognize

	erholen	recover
ge	gehören	belong
	gewinnen	win
miss	missbrauchen	abuse
	missverstehen	missunderstand
ver	vergessen	forget
	versprechen	promise
zer	zerbrechen	break
	zerstören	destroy
The underlined prefixes cover 95%		
of all inseparable verbs and		
you should keep them in mind.		

dual verbs		
prefix	examples	translation
durch	durchdringen (sep.)	penetrate
	durchfressen (insep.)	eat through
hinter	hinterlassen (sep.)	allow to s.o. to go behing
	hinterlassen (insep.)	leave
über	übersetzen (sep.)	ferry across
	übersetzen (insep.)	translate
um	umziehen (sep.)	change clothes
	umarmen (insep.)	hug
unter	untergehen (sep.)	sink
	unterbrechen (insep.)	interrupt
wider	widertönen (sep.)	echo
	widersprechen (insep.)	contradict
wieder	wiedersehen (sep.)	see again
	wiedergeben (insep.)	represent

We stress the prefix in separable verbs and the syllable after the prefix in inseparable verbs.

Example:
_U_mfahren (knock-down)   um f_a_hren (drive around)

Viel Erfolg